T0256906

Networks, Security and Complexity

This book is dedicated to my parents for supporting my prolonged education, and to my Aunt Margo and Uncle Fred for keeping me fed during it.

Networks, Security and Complexity

The Role of Public Policy in Critical Infrastructure Protection

Sean P. Gorman

George Mason University

Edward Elgar
Cheltenham, UK • Northampton, MA, USA

Published by
Edward Elgar Publishing Limited
Glensanda House
Montpellier Parade
Cheltenham
Glos GL50 1UA
UK

Edward Elgar Publishing, Inc.
136 West Street
Suite 202
Northampton
Massachusetts 01060
USA

A catalogue record for this book
is available from the British Library

Library of Congress Cataloguing in Publication Data
Gorman, S. P.
    Networks, security, and complexity : the role of public policy in critical
    infrastructure protection / Sean P. Gorman.
        p. cm.
    Includes bibliographical references.
    1. Computer security—United States. 2. Computer networks—Security
    measures—United States. 3. Terrorism—United States—Prevention. I. Title.

QA76.9.A25G657 2005
005.8—dc22   2005046195

ISBN 1 84376 952 2

Printed and bound in Great Britain by MPG Books Ltd, Bodmin, Cornwall

Contents

About the author

Sean P. Gorman was born on 2 May, 1974 in Austin, Texas. He graduated from Ramstein American High School, Ramstein, Germany in 1992. He received his Bachelor of Arts in International Studies and Political Science from Jacksonville University, Jacksonville, Florida in 1996. He then received his Master of Science in Geography from the University of Florida, Gainesville, Florida. He was posted at George Mason University's School of Public Policy as the Provost's High Potential research candidate. He was employed as adjunct faculty at American University's Kogod School of Business. He has also served as Vice President of Research and Development for a telecommunications mapping firm and was Director of Strategy for a Washington DC based technology incubator. His research is focused on cybersecurity and he works with the George Mason University Critical Infrastructure Protection Project. His cybersecurity research has been featured in the *Washington Post*, *Wired*, *Der Spiegel*, *Associated Press*, CNN, MSNBC, Fox, CNBC, and NPR. He has been published in *Telecommunications Policy*, *Environment and Planning A & B*, Tijdschrift voor Economische Geografie, *Journal of Crisis and Contingency Management*. He has also assisted the Homeland Security Advisory Council's Critical Infrastructure Task Force with modeling and simulation approaches to infrastructure and policy.

1. Setting the Stage

When two hijacked airliners slammed into the World Trade Center's twin towers on September 11th 2001, the view of America's vulnerability to foreign attack changed irrevocably. The country was devastated by the physical and symbolic destruction of economic critical infrastructure, as well as the massive loss of life that resulted. The obliteration of buildings and streets was obvious to any passerby, but below the street, vital fiber optic circuits were severed by the plummeting steel and concrete of the twin towers. These fibers not only handled voice phone calls, but also critical financial and communication processes underpinning the US economy.

Following the devastation of September 11th and the major collateral impacts on critical infrastructure in Manhattan, President Bush formed the Critical Infrastructure Protection Board, which was headed up by Richard Clarke. One of Clarke's first actions was to ask for a national map of infrastructure, 'an acupuncture map of the country so we will know where to harden our protection' (Yasin 2002, p.1). The National Infrastructure Simulation and Analysis center was tasked with creating 'a map of all the interdependent telecom and IT networks, gas pipelines, railroad systems, and electric power lines' (Yasin 2002, p.1).

By fortuitous circumstance, this was a map we had started several years back in 1997, and as we would soon discover, creating such a map had many repercussions. These repercussions came fully to light when the map and associated research was featured on the front page of the *Washington Post* in a story by Laura Blumenfeld, entitled, 'Dissertation Could be a Security Threat.' This book is about the research behind that map, what we learned from it, and its implications for public policy. The book also contains the substance of my dissertation for my doctorate from George Mason University's School of Public Policy.

When the story in the *Washington Post* came out, I was astonished by the amount of media attention it generated and the length of time it lasted. Media requests came in from most major news outlets and other places around the globe. In retrospect, I can understand how the story struck a nerve and created a cause for concern with many people. The *Post* story placed the research and map at the intersection of concern over terrorism and the security of the nation, and brought to light the clashing of those two concepts with American ideals like the freedom of information and academic inquiry. To understand the power of the map and why it raised such concern from a variety of people, both in the government and the private sector, it is useful to understand what comprises the map database. The database covers several broad critical infrastructures such as telecommunications, energy, banking and finance, transportation, and chemical sectors. Samples of the data in each sector include:

- Telecommunications – long haul fiber optic lines (over 30 carriers), metropolitan area network fiber optic lines (over 90 carriers), fiber lit buildings, colocation facilities, wire centers, wireless towers, Internet exchanges, submarine cable landings and routing, points of presence, carrier hotels, and tandem switches
- Energy – electric transmission line, electric substations, power plants, electric control area points and interconnections, service territories, electric market areas and interconnections, North American Electric Reliability Council (NERC) regions, electric transmission areas and interconnections, gas compressor stations, gas import/export points, gas pipelines, gas receipt and delivery points, gas storage facilities
- Banking and finance – location of federal financial institutions, brokerages, banks, Fedwire network operation centers and backups, Fedwire processing centers, Secure Financial Transaction Interchange interconnection points and fiber lines for the New York Stock Exchange and American Stock Exchange.
- Transportation – major roads and interstates, railroads, navigable waterways, strategic bridges and dams, docks and import/export points, tunnels, trans-shipment facilities.
- Chemical – hazardous material terminals and transportation routes, chemical and petro processing centers, intermodal facilities.

Using these data sets, we developed tools to identify vulnerabilities and interdependencies in the various infrastructures. This combination of tools and data was gleaned from public sources and developed by a small group of academicians, and therefore made many people uncomfortable.

The creation of the data and tools has generated two questions. Where did the data come from? Why was it collected? Since the 'where' is easier than the 'why', I'll address it first. The data was collected over seven years from a wide variety of sources. The one thing that all sources held in common was accessibility to the public. None of the data is proprietary in the form that we obtained it. Some data is no longer available publicly since the events of September 11th, but the vast majority can be purchased from third party vendors today. We acquired data from public utilities, municipalities, economic development agencies, planning and zoning commissions, network providers, government documents and reports, and third party spatial data providers.

Responding to the 'Why did we do it?' question requires a longer answer. It is also important to point out that by using 'we' and not 'I' throughout this introduction, I am referring to the many people who have been integral parts of the research. While all dissertations must be written by an individual, this research has been a team effort from its inception.

The research began as an attempt to create a map of the Internet and was part of a trend in a quickly evolving field of cybergeography. At that time the mapping of the Internet and the World Wide Web was shooting in several directions, ranging from Hal Burch and Bill Cheswick's traceroute maps of IP space, to cognitive images of a 3-D cyberspace. As a master's student in the department of geography at the University of Florida, I was interested in the physical geography of the Internet, and where the wires, routers, and other hardware were located. The pundits at the time were proclaiming that the Internet would bring the death of distance and the end of geography, although I knew that it had to have a physical location to wire up to the global village. Guided by my thesis advisor, Ed Malecki, I set out to try and start a map of the physical geography of the Internet. Without Ed's support and mentoring, I would have never continued in academia or have pursued this topic.

When we started the project, our hunch was that places were not being wired up equally and as a result there would be certain locations that were lacking in Internet connections, or were not connected at all. To put it succinctly, the Internet would not be the end of geography. It would merely be another infrastructure that would differentiate places, especially in terms of economic growth. Our map reinforced the hunch; there were vast differences between the connectivity of the most populated cities in the United States and other smaller cities (Malecki and Gorman 2001). We were not alone in this finding; several before and after us found similar results for a wide variety of Internet related phenomena.

While the finding alone was interesting, it started a more important activity: the creation of a physical Internet map and the making of connections to a number of researchers in the field of cybergeography. Three colleagues in particular, Martin Dodge, Anthony Townsend, and Matt Zook were invaluable collaborators who shared data and ideas to evolve the research. Martin, of the University College London, is the 'collector' and father of cybergeography through his website, www.cybergeography.org, and books, *Mapping Cyberspace* and the *Atlas of Cyberspace*. His tireless dissemination of research in the field and his cataloguing of cyberspace maps is invaluable to anyone interested in the subject area. Anthony Townsend, of New York University, was a groundbreaker in many areas of cybergeography, the first to map the location of domain registries, examine the connectivity of cities, conduct detailed investigations of metropolitan telecommunication infrastructure, and research the impacts of wireless and wifi on urban areas.   Finally, Matt Zook of Cal Berkley, and now a professor at the University of Kentucky, built a massive GIS[1] database of domain registry locations and also developed sophisticated bots for crawling the web to discover the location of a wide array of Internet activities, ranging from jobs on Monster.com to the production of adult content. Since the beginning of my research these three have been constant aides and collaborators for collecting data and sharing research and findings. Without any of the three the project would be greatly diminished. They are also a big part of the 'why the map was created', intellectual curiosity. It is not often in geography that the opportunity comes along to map something entirely new and that sense of adventure was a large impetus to the work.

Another major contribution to the mapping research came from Angela McIntee. Angela was another University of Florida Geography graduate student who worked with Ed Malecki after I graduated.   Angela and Ed continued the research we started at a much more granular level, beginning to collect the exact street locations of important Internet infrastructure, such as colocation facilities.   In the course of this research, Angela met a telecommunications executive named Dave Drazen who was fascinated by the work. At this point, the three of us (Angela, Dave and I) began work collecting detailed telecommunications infrastructure data for a variety of physical assets. We hoped to create data that would be useful to economic development agencies and real estate research firms. It was the spring of 2001, and terms like homeland security and critical infrastructure protection were not in the average American's lexicon.   The team laid a good groundwork of detailed data in a GIS format for many telecommunication infrastructures, especially for metropolitan area fiber.

That fall I started at George Mason University in hope of obtaining my PhD at their School of Public Policy. Heading into the PhD program I planned on researching global information networks, endeavoring to see if the same disparities we had found in the US occurred at the global level, and whether the structure of the network could be leveraged to help developing countries. A few weeks into the semester the tragedy of September 11th occurred, and while I did not realize it at the time, the course of my research shifted dramatically. At George Mason I began to work with many wonderful researchers who had spent years studying infrastructure networks, especially transportation.   Soon after arriving, a small and informal team consisting of Roger Stough, Laurie Schintler, and Raj Kulkarni developed. This team has been behind all the work I have been involved in since arriving at George Mason, and if this book were anything other than my dissertation, all three would be listed as co-authors. Roger provided invaluable leadership and support for the team, allowing us to focus on the research even before there was any support for it. Laurie was and is the director of the project, leading the team and lending us her considerable expertise in spatial statistics and network modeling. Raj is the genius behind the work, with a vast array of skills in geographic information systems, programming, physics, mathematics and network visualization – a modern day renaissance man.

The team soon found support from the newly formed Critical Infrastructure Protection Project at the George Mason School of Law. I had read online about the formation and funding of the center and thought we might be able to spin our physical infrastructure research into something that would be useful to the new research center. We typed up a quick two-page proposal and sent it over. Once the center was up and running we quickly heard from its new executive director John McCarthy. After presenting the work to John, we left with a good feeling, but never would have guessed what was about to happen next. A few days later, John sent an email asking if we would be available to give a presentation in downtown DC. A week later we found ourselves giving a briefing on our research to the White House's Office of Cybersecurity. We were stunned, and they were as well when we showed them the fiber lines lighting the very building where we were meeting. This presentation began a series of briefings to government agencies and stakeholders in the private sector. We strived to add something new to each briefing, and therefore, rapidly developed our tools and experiments. In the course of six months, John McCarthy and Kip Thomas navigated us through the web of big players in the field of critical infrastructure protection and cybersecurity. Without their guidance, we would have been swimming in uncharted waters. After the *Washington Post* story we met with even more agencies and stakeholders, many of which we had not even imagined would be interested.

The reactions to our research and findings were varied. Some said that if they had done the work it would be classified and never would have seen the light of day. Others said the laptop we used for the presentation should not be allowed to leave the building. Many were concerned with the fact that the data had come completely from open public sources, but some stated it was valuable data that the government had not been able to obtain to do their own vulnerability analysis. That is probably the greatest irony that we saw across our many interactions with the private sector and government. The private sector steadfastly refused to share data with the public sector, especially regarding vulnerabilities in their networks, and the government stated that they are hampered in doing vulnerability analysis without cooperation from private industry. Ironically, the vast majority of the data in question can be collected or purchased, thus our enemies could possibly have data that our own government does not. This of course has to be tempered by the idiom, 'you have to know what you do not know', and I do not know what lies in the classified world of the government and military. That said, if all the problems had been solved, I doubt it would continue to be a contentious issue.

While this was the biggest and most obvious issue I saw in the course of our research, many others remain. Is there a threat to our nation's critical infrastructure, especially cybersecurity? If there is a threat, what is truly critical in the nation's many infrastructure networks? How do we determine what is most critical? How are critical infrastructure networks interdependent and how do their resiliencies and vulnerabilities differ? If we have limited resources to protect critical networks, how can they best be invested? In an era of increasing technological homogeneity, can diversity and competition among network components increase our security from attack? These are some of the questions that our research, my dissertation, and this book will attempt to answer. The questions and approaches we developed resulted from more than two years of interaction with the government, private industry, and other academic researchers. The research had the benefit of evolving on the cusp of a new public policy issue with direct input and feedback from most of the critical government and private sector players involved in the topic. The book is focused on information infrastructure and its interdependencies, but many of the approaches and policy issues are generic to all critical infrastructures. The following chapter will provide the roadmap I followed in an attempt to put the research and context into a coherent piece of work.

NOTE

1. Geographic information system

2. Private Efficiencies and Public Vulnerabilities

Over the last two decades, the world has seen an emergence of new infrastructures, mainly due to advances in technology and the increasing pace of globalization. In addition to hard infrastructures such as roads, rail, and power networks, soft infrastructures such as fiber optic grids, wireless networks, and broadband to the home became vital to a new information economy. The emergence of an interconnected globe and the pervasiveness of information technologies have enabled an economic revolution. The information revolution is just one facet of an increasingly efficient economy, but has this drive for greater private efficiency and cost minimization resulted in public vulnerabilities[1] (Branscomb forthcoming, NRC 2002a)?   Could global dependence on critical information infrastructures be a vulnerability that is exploitable by hostile actors targeting the US or global economy? The reliance of the new economy on information has made the infrastructures that supply it critical to the functioning and stability of the nation.   The Critical Infrastructure Protection Board (CIPB) defines critical infrastructure as, 'the physical and cyber assets of public and private institutions residing in the following sectors: agriculture, food, water, public health, emergency services, government, defense industrial base, information and telecommunications, energy, transportation, banking and finance, chemicals and hazardous materials, and postal and shipping' (CIPB 2003, p.8). Providing adequate protection to these infrastructures is difficult due to the distributed control and nature of their operations. The problem is further compounded by the fact that private firms own 'most critical infrastructures' (CIPB 2003, p.17) and the objective of those firms is to minimize cost and maximize profitability, increasing efficiency.

'Cyberspace is their [all critical infrastructure] nervous system - the control system of our country' (CIPB 2002, p.8). Therefore, cyberspace, or more accurately, the Internet, lies at the core of critical infrastructure. The Internet links an amalgam of thousands of interconnected networks, and accomplishes this task in a very efficient manner. Some of these networks are vast global networks like MCI or Cable & Wireless, while others are small local networks, such as a university. Trying to provide a minimum level of security for all these networks is a daunting task, but one that has been increasingly highlighted as an area of importance for national security (CIPB 2002; NRC[2] 2002; NSTAC[3] 2002). The White House's National

Strategy to Secure Cyberspace states that, 'By 2002, our economy and national security are fully dependent upon information technology and the information infrastructure. A network of networks directly supports the operation of all sectors of our economy' (CIPB 2002, p.3).

The complexity and scale of the problem calls for innovative approaches. Recently, new theoretical advances have been made in understanding the fundamental structure and growth of complex networks (Watts and Strogatz 1998; Barabási and Albert 1999; Amaral et al. 2000). Researchers in several fields have begun investigating the structure of the complex interactions of networks that comprise the Internet (Faloutsos et al. 1999; Tangmunarunkit et al. 2002; Lakhina et al. 2002; Yook et al. 2001). Much of the work has revolved around the finding that the Internet at the autonomous system[4] (AS) and router levels forms a highly efficient network where a small minority of hubs have the vast majority of connections (Faloutsos et al. 1999; Albert and Barabási 2002). Further, while these types of networks are very resilient to random failures, they are very vulnerable to targeted attack (Albert et al. 2000; Callaway et al. 2000; Cohen et al. 2001). These findings lay a theoretical and empirically supported groundwork indicating that self-organizing competitive networks are highly efficient, but have the negative externality of systemic vulnerability.

The problems posed by critical infrastructure protection are highly interdependent and require an interdisciplinary approach. Information infrastructures, like the Internet, connect all sectors of the economy and society, and in turn are dependent on other critical sectors like fiber optic lines for transmission and electricity for power. In addition to the economic sectors and infrastructures, multiple disciplinary approaches are needed to analyze the issues involved. Physics and mathematics provide crucial understanding about the structure of networks, economics lends insights into efficiency trade-offs, geography often explains where infrastructure and economic activity are agglomerating, while public policy provides tools for taking action to help solve problems. The interdependent and interdisciplinary problems of critical infrastructure do not lend themselves well to the traditional analysis. Since there is just not one question to be answered, but instead a series of interconnected and interdependent questions, the problem needs to be reduced to a manageable set of issues. The challenge lies in creating a perspective that does not lose sight of the larger issues in which problems are nested.

This book is organized around four interconnected research questions that revolve around the larger question concerning the role of public policy in critical information infrastructure protection. To begin to answer the larger question, the following four smaller sets of research questions must be posed:

1. Are information infrastructure networks vulnerable? What is critical in these networks? What are the repercussions when critical segments of networks fail?
2. How are information networks different from other critical infrastructures like the electric power grid? Further, how are information infrastructures interdependent with other networks, especially from a spatial perspective?
3. If there are limited resources to protect a network, what is the most cost effective method of resource allocation? If those resources are public policies, how does one compare effectiveness of different policy strategies?
4. The protection of a network assumes that the nature of the attack is known, but how often is this true? At a macro level, how can policy help protect networks from unforeseen attacks?

In order to address these questions, the following structure is implemented. Chapter 3 addresses the question of whether there is a threat to critical infrastructure large enough to warrant public policy intervention. The methodology for the analysis in Chapter 3 is interpretive. Chapter 4 reviews the extensive literature surrounding critical information infrastructure protection. This literature includes the economics of agglomeration, the geography of information infrastructure, the mathematical structure of networks, and public policy approaches to information infrastructure protection (i.e. cybersecurity). Chapter 4 also describes the research problems and the hypotheses to be covered by the book. Chapters 5, 6, 7, and 8 diverge from traditional academic format by treating each chapter as a separate research problem addressing one of the four research questions posed above, with its own methodology, analysis, results, and conclusions. Chapter 9 provides conclusions and addresses the broader question: 'Are private efficiencies creating public vulnerabilities?'

NOTES

1. The term and concept 'private efficiencies creating public vulnerabilities' came from discussions with Lewis Branscomb and Phil Auerswald. They coined the phrase, and it has been borrowed for this research.
2. National Research Council
3. National Security Telecommunications Advisory Committee

4. For practical purposes, ASs can be individual firms connected to the Internet. Often as a result of merger and acquisition, large firms consist of several ASs.

3. Is there a Threat?

Before endeavoring to identify critical vulnerabilities in the nation's critical information infrastructure and to look for defenses, one must answer the question: 'is there a threat, and if so, what is it?' Green (2002) maintains that there is a 'myth' of cyberterrorism in the current administration:

> There is no such thing as cyberterrorism - no instance of anyone ever having been killed by a terrorist (or anyone else) using a computer. Nor is there compelling evidence that Al Qaeda or any other terrorist organization has resorted to computers for any sort of serious destructive activity (p.1).

Berinato (2002) extends the argument, stating that terrorist organizations like Al Qaeda will follow the path of least resistance. Being a cheaper and easier alternative to cyber attacks, physical attacks offer just that. Even the use of cyber attacks to control physical infrastructure electronic systems has only been considered a worst-case scenario, causing minor inconvenience. These reports have largely been from investigative reporters relying on interviews with 'experts' in the field, like Georgetown University Professor Dorothy Denning, 'Not only does [cyberterrorism] not rank alongside chemical, biological, or nuclear weapons, but it is not anywhere near as serious as other potential threats like car bombs or suicide bombers,' (Green 2002, p. 2).

A more analytic approach was taken by the United States Naval War College who, in conjunction with Gartner Research, simulated a 'digital Pearl Harbor' attack against the nation's critical infrastructures. The study found that 'a group of hackers couldn't single-handedly bring down the United States' national data infrastructure, but a terrorist team would be able to do significant localized damage to U.S. systems' (Kane 2002, p.1).

The results had a further caveat that such an attack would require $200 million in funding, country-level intelligence and five years of preparation time. Whether there is an enemy that could undertake such an offensive is an open question. Is there a realistic national security threat posed by critical infrastructure and cybersecurity, or is it a myth that has been oversold for various reasons? To date, most available evidence of cyber threats in the public domain is anecdotal. It is useful, though, to examine the anecdotal evidence of critical infrastructure threats. To provide some structure to the wide range of types of attack considered, they are divided into physical failures, unintentional and intentional, and malicious cyber attacks and developing cyber warfare capabilities.

ATTACK OF THE BACKHOES AND MASSIVE PHYSICAL TELECOM FAILURES

While cyber attacks tend to get the majority of media coverage, it is also important to note critical infrastructure damage caused by physical failures. Physical failures in the telecommunications grid are probably the most frequent on a day-to-day basis, resulting largely from accidental fiber cuts from backhoes and shovels. The prevalence of accidental fiber cuts can be seen in the number of local 'call before you dig' and 'Miss Utility' programs. While most of these cuts result in minor inconveniences like the loss of localized service, several cuts have resulted in major outages. Fiber cuts have often plagued airport air traffic control. In 1990, a severed fiber shut down Chicago's O'Hare airport. The following year, a cable cut in New Jersey shut down all three New York airports and caused air traffic control problems from DC to Boston (Neuman 1991). Fiber cuts can also reveal the interdependency of several critical infrastructures: the same fiber cut that shut down New York City's airports also shut down the NY Mercantile Exchange and hampered long-distance calling for nine hours (Neuman 1991). Further, fiber cuts can often be time consuming to repair: in 2000 a San Jose cut left customers out of service for over a week, 'The repair work is mind-numbingly tedious, with each wire having to be spliced by hand and then tested' (Neuman 2000). More recently a train derailment and chemical spill in Baltimore's Howard St. Tunnel slowed down Internet traffic from coast-to-coast. While the robust SONET ring technology employed by several providers who lost circuits did reroute traffic quickly, the flood of rerouted traffic along poorly capacitated alternative routes slowed down traffic as far away as Seattle and Los Angeles (Lindstrom 2001). More recently there were three unrelated fiber cuts on May 20th 2004 in Southern Utah, Ashburn, VA, and the Fort Worth area of Texas that all caused outages for 911 emergency services along with other entities reliant on the severed fiber[1]. The Utah cut was caused by a construction company, the Texas cut by a road improvement project, and the Virginia cut by a commercial lawnmower. All three cuts were single points of failure.

THE IMPACT OF TELECOMMUNICATIONS FAILURE DURING 9/11

The single largest physical loss of telecommunications infrastructure was the fall of the World Trade Center towers on 9/11. FCC records report that Verizon alone had to replace 1.5 million voice circuits, 4.4 million data circuits, and 19 SONET rings. In addition, 112,000 private branch exchange trunks, and 11,000 fiber lines dedicated to Internet service providers were destroyed (FCC 2001, GAO 2003). Further, Verizon lost its primary central office, 140 West St., resulting in the loss of telecommunication service to 34,000 businesses, including the New York financial district (GAO 2002). The loss of the Bank of New York's primary data center caused nearly $80 billion in securities trades to fail (Newman 2002). Following the destruction of 9/11, the Federal government's calls for firms to locate backup facilities 120 miles from Manhattan were rejected by the financial community; therefore, most vulnerabilities are considered still to be unfixed (GAO 2002, Newman 2002). The vulnerabilities of fiber diversity have been well noted by the government as early as 1995:

> The use of optical fiber increases the effects of strategic sabotage attacks because optical fiber technology is diminishing the number of geographic transmission routes, increasing the concentration of traffic within those routes, reducing the use of other transmission technologies and restricting spatial diversity (NIST 1995, p. 23).

While there have only been a few documented cases of fiber sabotage, their effect has been dramatic. Over the past two years, the Seattle area has been plagued by a fiber saboteur who has taken out 911 services four times with strategic fiber cuts (Halsne 2003). The most recent cut on 3 September, 2003 disabled 911 services for nearly 9 hours. The perpetrator remains at large (Halsne 2003).

There is often a somewhat mistaken belief that fiber networks are fully redundant rings that would prevent these types of cuts from disrupting critical resources. In a 5 August, 2003 court case involving the Maine Public Utility Commission, an expert witness from Verizon stated that only 10 percent of the fiber rings in Maine are fully redundant, and the remaining 90 percent are at least partially collapsed and vulnerable to single cut failures (Maine PUC, 2003). The standard operating procedure for restoring a failed line is to locate the lead engineer for the region, consult paper maps, manually identify an alternative route, and send technicians to wire jumper around the outage (Maine PUC, 2003). The reason that collapsed circuits are used is to save cost – it is more expensive to utilize fully redundant rings. The use of collapsed SONET rings is another striking example of private efficiencies resulting in public vulnerabilities. While the difficulties imposed by dependence on telecommunications fiber and anecdotes of fiber failures are well documented, there has been little organized effort to quantify the impact of the vulnerability at a national level.

LIGHTS OUT

Telecommunication networks are not the only critical infrastructure prone
to physical failures. While physical telecommunication failures may be the
most common, electrical power grid failures are by far the most obvious to
the public. While the huge Northeast blackout on 14 August, 2003 is one of
the largest and most recent, it is far from singular:

> On August 10th, 1996, faults in Oregon at the Keeler-Allston 500 kV line and the
> Ross-Lexington 230 kV line resulted in excess load. This, in turn, triggered the
> tripping of generators at McNary Dam, causing 500 MW oscillations, which
> caused the separation of the North-South Pacific intertie near the California-
> Oregon border. This led to islanding and blackouts in 11 U.S. states and 2
> Canadian provinces and was estimated to cost $1.5 billion to $2 billion and
> included all aspects of interconnected infrastructures (Amin 2001, p. 22).

The 1996 outage was caused inadvertently by sagging power lines
shorting when they came in contact with untrimmed trees. Other large-scale
power outages include the northeast blackouts of 1977 and 1965. Since the
outage of 2003 is the most recent, it warrants a closer look into its causes
and effects. The conditions during the 1996 and 2003 blackout were quite
similar, as both occurred during August when power consumption, along
with the summer heat, is at a peak. In the 1996 outage, over-capacitated
lines resulted in a cascading failure that spread throughout the region. In
the case of the 2003 outage, the series of events began when FirstEnergy's
Eastlake coal generation plant tripped off, sending a puff of ash spewing
into the local neighborhood. An hour after the coal plant failure, the
Chamberlin to Harding power line tripped, causing the power to be rerouted
to the Hanna to Juniper line (PSERC 2003). Because energy in an electric
power grid cannot be stored or slowed down, it must be immediately routed
to alternative paths in the network. Under conditions of high utilization of
power lines, there is no excess capacity to absorb the rerouted power from a
failed line, thus the alternative paths fail. This sequence can be the start of a
domino effect, cascading power throughout the network and causing an
entire grid failure. This is the scenario that caused the 2003 blackout. The
Hanna to Juniper line could not absorb the rerouted power from the failed
Chamberlin to Harding line, and the load caused it to sag and short on a tree
limb. The Hanna failure initiated wild swings of rerouted power as the grid
strained to absorb the failures. However, after interconnects with American
Electric Power Co. failed, power lines and power plants around the
Northeast tripped off, causing the regional blackout (PSERC 2003). The

effect of the blackout can be seen in satellite images of the Northeast before
and during the blackout (Figures 3.1 and 3.2).

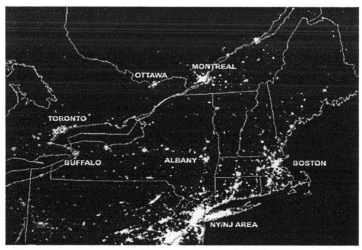

Source: Platts Inc.

*Figure 3.1   13 August, 2003 satellite image of Northeast US and Canada
prior to the blackout*

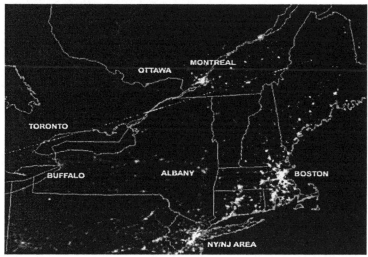

Source: Platts Inc.

Figure 3.2   14 August, 2003 satellite image during the blackout

The 2003 blackout also poignantly illustrated the interdependencies between the US's power network and Internet infrastructure. As power failed, many regional and enterprise networks experienced outages, although most national backbone networks had adequate backup power supplies to survive the outage (Renesys 2003). The scope of network outages can be clearly seen in Figure 3.3, which illustrates the Internet routing outages during the blackout.

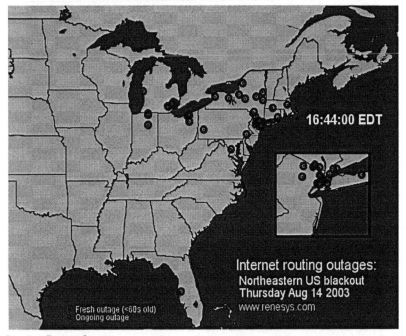

Source: Renesys Inc.

Figure 3.3   Internet routing outages during the 2003 blackout

While the majority have pointed to faults in FirstEnergy's power grid as the cause of the August blackout, it has not escaped the scrutiny of conspiracy theorists connecting it to Al Qaeda. Coincidental evidence, such as the fact that Egypt has the same SCADA vendor as the systems involved in the blackout, and North American Electric Reliability Council (NERC) files suggesting that a January 2003 cyber attack was a dry run on the power grid, has been used to make a weak case for terrorist involvement (Wilson 2003). More sound evidence of power grid sabotage was revealed in the FBI's arrest of a man in Sacramento, CA for dismantling 10 power grid towers through the Western United States (Lerten 2003). The arrested man claims he carried out the acts to point out vulnerabilities in the network.

HOLLYWOOD CYBER ATTACKS

The public perception of cyber attacks often takes its lead from Hollywood's imagination, 'doomsday scenarios in which terrorists hijack nuclear weapons, airliners, or military computers from halfway around the world' (Green 2002). While perception can outpace even Hollywood, the pantheon of real world cyber attacks often matches the movies in imagination, if not actual impact. Cyber attacks have become increasingly sophisticated and the individuals behind them are often not juvenile hackers, but organized crime syndicates and nation state actors. Tracking cyber attacks and discovering the culprits is incredibly difficult and rarely accomplished, but the few successes and best guesses expose some disturbing trends. The following brief case studies are intended to illustrate the sophistication of attacks, their economic motivations, and their possible implications for national security.

Millions of packets flood through a data pipe into a major Manhattan bank, crashing upon the firewall acting as the bank's first line of defense. The tidal wave of packets overwhelms the firewall's ability to sort the traffic, shutting it down and denying any traffic entry to the bank network. The attack causes a temporary network outage, but on the surface has not violated the security of the network. Hidden in the flood of packets that saturated the firewall was a packet sniffer, which acts as a traffic spy gathering data unbeknown to the network administrator. When the network administrator goes to reinitialize the downed firewall, the packet sniffer grabs his/her user name and password and passes it along to the bank's unknown assailants. Money is then withdrawn from the compromised bank and sent to a second bank, and then sent to a third or fourth bank. By the time the breach has been discovered (typically a two-hour window of operation) the money has been withdrawn from the final bank, and the transfer is recognized as a valid transaction. Only the intervening and originating bank created and authorized the fraudulent transfer, thus the terminating bank is not held liable. The monetary loss is covered by insurance and the system continues to operate. 'Successful and unsuccessful attacks like one just described happen on a daily basis throughout the financial community'[2], according to one veteran security executive. Perhaps the most disturbing aspect of this attack was that the forensic investigation afterwards revealed that the perpetrator was a nation state testing the method as a means of attack on the solvency of financial infrastructure. The majority of cyber bank attacks are tightly screened from public attention by strict non-disclosure agreements in the name of maintaining public confidence.

THE RUSSIAN CONNECTION

While the above incident comes from an undisclosed source and cannot be verified, there are growing public accounts of cyber attacks, which are increasingly linked with Russian organized crime. The growing problem of Russian cybercrime and the resulting financial loss led the FBI (2001) to issue a public warning about, 'organized hacker groups from Eastern Europe, specifically Russia and the Ukraine' exploiting Microsoft vulnerabilities for financial gain. Russian organized crime has been blamed by various media outlets for a stream of high profile cyber attacks, 'stealing secret Microsoft source codes, ransacking the Pentagon's computers, hacking into NATO military websites, posting thousands of credit card numbers on the Internet, and stealing millions of dollars from Western banks' (Lunev 2001, p.1).

Specifics that outline targets and actors in cyber attacks are often difficult to come by. The few cases that have actually been prosecuted offer insight into the nature of these operations. In 2001, the FBI arrested two Russian hackers by tricking them into coming to the United States for job interviews with security firms and hacking into their computers for evidence. While the Russian government protested about the tactics employed by the FBI, the two hackers were tried and convicted in a US court. The court cases revealed some interesting details about the hackers' methods and targets. The Russian pair first hacked into CTS Network services to launch attacks on two credit card processing centers, Sterling Microsystems and Transmark, while also stealing financial data from Los Angeles-based NaraBank and FSI Inc. The second part of their strategy was breaking into Glen Rock Financial Service, and then threatening the exposure of credit card information if the company did not pay a ransom (DOJ 2001). Hacking and extortion techniques have been frequent tactics employed by Russian organized crime, the most prominent being the theft of 300,000 credit cards from CD Universe, which were then held for ransom (Lunev 2001). Reports maintain that Moscow houses the Civil Hacker School, which is funded by Russian intelligence agencies and Russian crime syndicates to ensure a steady supply of cybercrime talent (Lunev 2001). This supposed investment in developing cyber manpower seems to have paid off in the increasing sophistication of cyber attacks.

THE WEEK OF INTERNET PREDATORS

Possibly the best example of the growing weight and sophistication of cyber attacks on the Internet was the multiple attacks that occurred across the Internet in mid-August of 2003. The first attack was the Lovesan worm, which started on 11 August, 2003 and attacked Windows XP and Windows 2000 operating systems with an executable file that randomly turns off the affected computer. Three different mutations of the worm infected hundreds of thousands of computers. Lovesan was followed by the Nachi worm, which used the same strategy to affect Microsoft IIS 5.0 servers. In a twist, the Nachi worm killed the Lovesan worm and patched the vulnerability that allowed the Lovesan worm to propagate. This caused a tremendous amount of Internet traffic, which overwhelmed and shut down many networks, including the world's largest Intranet, which belonged to the US Navy and Marine Corp (Messmer 2003). The third of the disastrous trio was the Sobig.F virus, which spread through Microsoft Windows email. The address from which the email arrived was spoofed with domain names associated with the end-user. When the attachment was downloaded it executed a program that told the affected computer to download a program from 20 different servers located across the USA, Europe and Korea. The virus was also recorded to open proxies on affected machines, allowing them to be used as Spam (unsolicited bulk commercial email) gateways to the Internet. Eventually the big three predators spawned scavenger predators like the Dumaru virus, which sends a phony email from support@microsoft.com, indicating that it has a patch for the Lovesan worm. The attachment leaves a backdoor into the affected computer allowing it to be remotely controlled.

Not only does the latest round of cyber attacks illustrate a higher level of sophistication than just hacking incidents, it also illustrates an increasing level of impact. Detailed analysis of the attacks has uncovered some disturbing implications. Peter Simpson, manager of ThreatLab at Clearswift, maintains that the Sobig virus was developed by organized crime syndicates to facilitate Spam scams (Sturgeon 2003). Viruses like Sobig leave backdoors, or Trojan horses, on computers which allow them to be remotely controlled at a later date. Most often these backdoors are used to send Spam so that the unsolicited mail cannot be filtered out as coming from previously known Spammer addresses. Analysis by Sandvine Inc. found that 80 percent of all Spam is sent through hijacked home computers (Leyden 2004). While Spam is annoying, it hardly seems to constitute a high level threat of any sort. This concept is beginning to change, as more evidence is uncovered. One of the latest discoveries reveals the utilization of these backdoors in a sophisticated credit card fraud scheme, again linked to the Russian underworld. Computers that have been remotely controlled by virus and worm-enabled backdoors are linked in a ring, with each computer hosting a porn site for a few seconds before passing it off to another site. The ring also rotates compromised computers to send Spam, directing surfers to the websites (GRID 2003). The sites then swipe unsuspecting customers' credit card numbers. A similar plot by a group of Polish hackers uses virus-enabled backdoors to route traffic through compromised computers, so that cybercrime activities cannot be traced. They offer the service to Spammers, purveyors of Internet fraud, and other nefarious groups as a form of invisible hosting (McWilliams 2003). The same Polish group also offers for sale the use of 450,000 hijacked computers with high-speed connections for a variety of illicit activities. There is a growing black market for hijacked computers that can be used for everything from Spam to distributed denial of service techniques.

What is critical to understand about the growing threat of Spam is not the actual email, but the economic incentive it has created. Spam has produced an arms race between the network providers setting up increasingly sophisticated filtering and blocking mechanisms and Spammers continually adapting and innovating to circumvent those defenses. As illustrated above, one of Spam's primary tactics has been the use of worms and viruses to hijack home computers and then route Spam through them. The result is that there is now an economic incentive to develop increasingly sophisticated worms and viruses, where there was not one before. The by-product of this economic incentive is that there is now a market for hijacked machines, and the groups operating the market are not of the law-abiding variety. Currently there are millions of hijacked high-speed computers available for hire around the globe. Further, these computers are remotely controlled, untraceable and scattered across many jurisdictions.

At the same time the number of hijacked machines for hire is increasing, and the number of vulnerabilities that can be exploited by denial of service attacks is also increasing. It is not hard to imagine a globally distributed and coordinated denial of service attack utilizing thousands of hijacked machines on a wide variety of critical infrastructure targets. In the past, denial of service attacks have been curtailed by the lack of attack resources, as in the attack on the root name servers in October of 2002, or the threat of being caught, as in the case of the Mafia Boys attack in May 2000. As a result of the technological shift caused by Spam this is no longer the case. Spam is now a threat that should garner more attention by those concerned about critical infrastructure protection.

Are cyber attacks from organized crime syndicates and Spam a national security issue? Do they constitute cyber terrorism? The cyber terrorism question is a matter of definition, but a reasonable case can be made that organized crime does play a role in funding and equipping terrorist groups. The academic literature and news reports indicate a strong linkage between organized crime, cyber crime, and the funding and growth of terrorist groups (Bequai 2002; Philippsohn 2001; Furnell and Warren 1999; Lunev 2001). Many of the cyber attack techniques outlined above have been directly linked to funding terrorist groups, including Spam/porn, credit card theft, identity fraud, and money laundering (Bequai 2002). There have also been reports of connections between Russian organized crime and Al Qaeda in the appropriation of weapons of mass destruction and the utilization of Al Qaeda operatives in Russian apartment bombings (Lunev 2001; Getz 2001). While the majority of evidence often comes from unverified news reports, the existence of growing cyber attack capacity in Russian and other organized crime syndicates is without doubt. Further, the connection between these crime syndicates and terrorist organizations is well documented. At a minimum, the growing rate of cyber attacks and related financial crime is funding terrorist groups and it would not be difficult to believe terrorist groups are considering evolving cyber attack tactics to aid their own missions. Both aspects point to cybersecurity as an area of increasing importance to national security.

AL QAEDA AS A CYBER THREAT

The analysis so far has examined critical infrastructure and cybersecurity as the focus of a general security threat with circumstantial connections to terrorism. The vulnerability of critical infrastructure is well documented from actual failures, and the sophistication of growing malicious cyber attacks has been laid out, but are these areas that Al Qaeda are looking to exploit? Al Qaeda's connection to the technical skills to implement infrastructure attacks appears to be in place, but as stated before, no terrorist has ever used a computer to kill a person. Further, Al Qaeda and other terrorist groups have always used physical attacks focused on inflicting the loss of human life to force world attention to their causes. Without precedent, is there evidence that is compelling enough to take serious precautions against a cyber threat that has yet to have occurred?

A good place to start is by examining Al Qaeda's own rhetoric on the matter. On 27 December, 2001 Osama Bin Laden put out a statement asserting that, 'It is very important to concentrate on hitting the US economy through all possible means' (Verton 2003 p. xv). This statement has become a mantra within Al Qaeda to focus on striking the 'key pillars' of the US economy. Quoting this communiqué by Bin Laden, Al Qaeda's Abu Hafs Brigade claimed responsibility for the August 2003 Northeast blackout (Al-Hayat 2003). While post-blackout analysis and statements by the Bush administration ruled out any terrorist involvement, the statement does make clear the attention Al Qaeda has focused on critical infrastructures and the US economy's dependence on them. The Al Qaeda statement went on to state that the goal of the supposed blackout attack was:

> hitting the major pillar of the U.S. economy (the Stock Exchange)…[and] the UN, which is opposed to Islam, and is based in New York. It is a message to all the investors that the U.S. is no longer a safe country for their money, knowing that the U.S. economy greatly relies on the trust of the investor (Al-Hayat 2003, p. 2).

While the statement was most likely opportunist propaganda, it does point to an evolution in the strategies and tactics of Al Qaeda. It appears that Al Qaeda has come to believe that targeting the US economy can have a very damaging effect. Further, the US economy's reliance on vulnerable critical infrastructures makes these easy targets. Last, guerilla attacks and tactics on these infrastructures will erode public confidence, thereby having a devastating long-term impact on the US economy. Statements by Al Qaeda paint critical infrastructure as a strategic target, but does Al Qaeda intend to use cyber tactics for possible attacks? In an interview with Dan Verton (2003), Sheikh Omar Bakri Muhammad, the leader of Al Qaeda-connected al-Muhajirun, stated that, 'In a matter of time, you will see attacks on the stock market' (p.84). Bakri expands this statement by outlining how such an attack might go forward and how resources are being developed to do so, 'I would not be surprised if tomorrow I hear of a big economic collapse because of somebody attacking the main technical systems in big companies. There are millions of Muslims around the world involved in hacking the Pentagon and Israeli government sites' (p.84). Finally, the Sheikh concludes his statement with, 'I would advise those who doubt Al Qaeda's interest in cyber weapons to take Osama Bin Laden very seriously. The third letter from Osama Bin Laden a few months ago was clearly addressing using the technology in order to destroy the economy of capitalist states' (p.85).

While the statements of Sheikh Bakri are definitive, one wonders how much of the statement is inflammatory rhetoric to promote Al Qaeda's cause and how much is actual threat. According to a special report on Internet Security by *The Economist* (2003), American intelligence uncovered an Al Qaeda hideout in Pakistan that had been used to train hackers to attack the computer systems of power grids, dams and nuclear plants. While none of this is a smoking gun, it does point to a growing threat that US policy would be ill advised not to prepare for.

CYBER WARFARE AND THE NATION STATE

Perhaps an even stronger argument for including both cybersecurity and critical infrastructure as integral aspects of national security is the growing cyber warfare threat posed by nation states. Conservative reports indicate that 20 to 30 countries are developing or already possess cyber warfare capabilities (Vegh 2002). The growing dependence of nation states on information technology for economic viability and military capabilities, has led to grandiose statements such as: 'cyberspace has become a new international battlefield. Whereas military victories used to be won through physical confrontation of weapons and soldiers, the information warfare being waged today involves computer sabotage by hackers acting on the behalf of private interests of governments' (Adams 2001, p. 98).

Cyber warfare itself dates back to the cold war, when Sandia laboratories traced virus attacks on US computers and found them to originate from Bulgaria and East Germany (Guttman and Elburg 2002). Malicious attacks against Department of Defense computers have risen from 225 in 1994 to 40,000 in 2001 (Vegh 2002). Perhaps the most widespread and damaging attacks occurred in March 1998; code named 'Moonlight Maze' they resulted in the theft of 'thousands of files containing technical research, contracts, encryption techniques, and unclassified but essential data relating to the Pentagon's war-planning systems' (Adams 2001, p.99). Red-teaming exercises that tested the strength of US computer defenses, such as 'Eligible Receiver' and 'Zenith Star' illuminated several vulnerabilities including the ability to shut off the power grids of nine cities, control the 911 emergency systems, and 'paralyze' military command and control systems (Adams 2001). Many skeptics point out that there has been no hard evidence of foreign government involvement in any cyber attack (Vegh 2002). The ability to mask the origin of an attack makes the possibility of ever producing hard evidence unlikely, but there are other avenues to investigate the role of nation states in cyber attacks.

CHINA'S CYBER SOLDIERS

The most well documented cyber warfare initiative belongs to China, which has been conducting cyber warfare exercises since 1997 and has been operating an information warfare military unit since 2000 (McDonald 2003). The ability to wage cyber warfare with information technologies is considered to be a critical component of China's national strength (Yoshihara 2001). The growth and reach of China's information warfare capabilities is impressive, including the establishment of a cyber warfare complex in Bejucal, Cuba, to monitor data traffic and intercept US communications (McDonald 2003). Security experts state that Chinese hackers are probing and mapping critical US systems, especially financial networks, on a daily basis[3]. The gravity of these capabilities becomes more disturbing when placed in the context of Chinese military strategy documents. The release of *Unrestricted Warfare* provides an interesting perspective on the development of China's cyber warfare capabilities. The book proposes tactics for developing countries, in particular China, to compensate for their military inferiority vis-à-vis the United States during a high-tech war (Liang and Xiangsui 1999). The document reveals a strategy of asymmetric warfare that uses non-traditional tactics to defeat a military superior foe (explicitly the US):

> As we see it, a single man-made stock-market crash, a single computer virus invasion, or a single rumor or scandal that results in a fluctuation in the enemy country's exchange rates or exposes the leaders of an enemy country on the Internet, all can be included in the ranks of new-concept weapons (Liang and Xiangsui 1999, p. 44).

> ...in the information age, the influence exerted by a nuclear bomb is perhaps less than the influence exerted by a hacker (Liang and Xiangsui 1999, p. 47).

While few would argue in current times that a hacker of even the most sophisticated cyber warfare capabilities matches the threat of a nuclear weapon, it is clear that elements of the Chinese military see it as the future and are investing heavily in that future.

Investment in cyber capabilities may not be confined to military expenditures. Since the telecommunications collapse of 2001, Chinese buyers have purchased PSINet, Level 3, Asia Global Crossing, and Global Crossing Inc., a total original US investment of $20 billion purchased for 3 cents on the dollar by various Chinese interests (Fonow 2003). Robert Fonow of the National Defense University (2003) believes these Chinese acquisitions could provide a platform for espionage and network warfare, citing that 95 percent of Department of Defense traffic uses the international telecommunications system. With the Chinese telecom acquisitions listed above, most military and diplomatic traffic would pass over Chinese-owned networks, with some traffic passing through facilities in the Chinese mainland (Fonow 2003). The overriding belief is that China plans to use its cyber warfare capabilities to prevent the projection of US force by preventing command and control apparatuses that guarantee supply lines and troop coordination (Fonow 2003). In fact many of these same tactics were employed with a high level of success by the US military in the invasion of Iraq to render the enemy immobile. A combination of such tactics in conjunction with disruptions of the domestic financial system paints a bleak, if hypothetical picture.

ANALYSIS

Green (2002) in his *Washington Monthly* article is correct that terrorists cannot kill people with computers and further that no one has been killed by hacking or even cyber warfare incidents. Just because lapses in cybersecurity have not resulted in bloodshed, should not prevent it from being an issue of importance to national security. Terrorists have not used nuclear weapons to kill anyone either, but that does not prevent the possibility from being a topic of grave concern. Green and others do make a valid point that the hype and hyperbole of threat and reality do need to be investigated analytically. This short synopsis of catalogued events and evidence is an attempt to lay out what cases have been documented and what directions current trends could realistically take. Critical information infrastructure has two fundamental components, the physical fiber and devices, and the data and systems that run over them, roughly broken in physical and cyber. Physical infrastructure is the less studied of the two but the impacts of random and planned failures exhibit significant impacts on areas as diverse as financial systems and air traffic control. While there is a consensus that physical failures can have very damaging results, there is little understanding of what parts of the infrastructure are most vulnerable or how to quantify what needs to be protected and the cost justification.

The area of cyber vulnerabilities is better documented and has many more cases of actual exploitation, but it also lacks thorough analysis of protection strategies and cost-benefit analysis, especially in the realm of policy. The growing sophistication of cyber attacks points to a rapidly growing threat that has moved beyond simple web defacements and the motivations of teenagers hacking for fun. There is mounting evidence of cyber attacks being orchestrated by organized crime syndicates with documented connections to terrorist organizations. Further, there is growing evidence of nation states becoming heavily involved in developing cyber attack capabilities. The nature of both threats points to a fundamental understanding of information infrastructure as an area of critical national security.

JURISDICTION OF CRITICAL INFORMATION INFRASTRUCTURE

In the aftermath of 9/11 critical infrastructure protection came to the fore in the US government, and telecommunication and cybersecurity became one of the most immediately identifiable areas of focus. Currently the security of the nation's telecommunications system, which is in vast part controlled by private interests, falls under several federal jurisdictions. Unlike the financial sector there is not a firm regulatory body or framework when it comes to the security aspects of telecommunications. In general telecommunications falls under the FCC (Federal Communications Commission), but when it comes to security the federal mandate becomes less clear. The White House's National Communication System (NCS) was created for coordinating and planning the telecommunications sector to support crises and disasters. This role has grown since the agency's inception in 1962 to include the security of telecommunications infrastructure, as well as the Internet. Under the Clinton administration, the White House's Critical Infrastructure Protection Board was also formed to look after the security of the nation's core infrastructure including telecommunications, and its former head, Richard Clarke, was the federal government's cybersecurity czar. Agencies such as the Federal Reserve Bank and Department of the Treasury and Justice have also become involved in telecommunications security when it is an integral part of their domains as in the case of financial services and their related networks.

The creation of the Department of Homeland Security has again changed this landscape somewhat. On 1 March, 2003 the NCS moved into the new Department of Homeland Security under the Information Analysis and Infrastructure Protection (IAIP) Directorate. According to the President's fiscal budget, $4.2 billion will be spent on cybersecurity in 2003 and $4.5 billion has been requested to protect critical infrastructure (Dean 2002, Green 2002).

There is undeniable government action in the area, but to assess the effectiveness of that action one must first develop an understanding of the economic forces that have caused such a large dependency on information infrastructure in the US. Knowledge of the mathematical characteristics of the large complex networks formed by information infrastructure is also a prerequisite. The literature on the growth of the information economy, followed by the literature of network complexity and mathematics is covered next in an attempt to lay such a foundation.

NOTES

1. Archived from North American Network Operator Group Mailing List (www.nanog.org)
2. Discussions with a security executive who requested anonymity, 5 April, 2003
3. Discussions with a security executive who requested anonymity, 5 April, 2003

4. Literature Review of Conceptual Framework

If one accepts the fact that there is a threat to the US's information infrastructure, then it becomes necessary to understand where and why the infrastructure is vulnerable. To begin to grapple with these questions several publications need to be surveyed in order to examine the premise: do private efficiencies result in public vulnerabilities? The fundamental idea behind this premise is that in order to gain efficiencies, private firms will agglomerate economic activity, especially high order activities such as command and control. These agglomerations will occur in large metropolitan areas in order to take advantage of skilled labor and economies of scale and scope. Information infrastructure will also agglomerate in the same large metropolitan areas to meet demand, creating efficient information hubs. The efficient hub networks formed by information infrastructure are vulnerable to targeted attack; without the hubs the network will become disconnected.

In order to support this premise evidence will be drawn from a range of literature. Regional economics will provide support for the spatial agglomeration of economic activity in large metropolitan areas, encapsulated in the theory of global cities. Next, the geographic literature of information networks will be covered to establish that information infrastructure is also agglomerating in the same metropolitan areas to provide economic command and control capabilities. Theoretical support for the use of agglomeration and hubbing to increase efficiency will be gained from an examination of the physics and mathematics literature regarding the structure of complex networks. This literature will also illustrate how one of the trade-offs of network efficiency is vulnerability to targeted attacks on hubs, the public vulnerability created by private efficiency. Finally the policy literature on critical infrastructure protection and cybersecurity will be covered. First, a conceptual and operational definition of critical infrastructure is provided.

DEFINING CRITICAL INFRASTRUCTURE

Before establishing the theory upon which this research is based, it is useful to define what is meant by critical infrastructure and to define what aspects of critical infrastructure this book will endeavor to understand. We start first with the definition of infrastructure.

The President's Commission on Critical Infrastructure Protection (PCCIP) defines infrastructure as, 'a network of independent, mostly privately-owned, man-made systems and processes that function collaboratively and synergistically to produce and distribute a continuous flow of essential goods and services' (PCCIP 1997 as cited in Rinaldi et al. 2001).

Within this definition of infrastructure, the commission further delineated that critical infrastructures were those 'whose incapacity or destruction would have a debilitating impact on our defense and economic security' (PCCIP 1997 as cited in Rinaldi et al. 2001). The PCCIP's initial work evolved into the current set of critical infrastructures as delineated by the President's Critical Infrastructure Protection Board to include the physical and cyber assets of public and private institutions residing in the following sectors: agriculture, food, water, public health, emergency services, government, defense industrial base, information and telecommunications, energy, transportation, banking and finance, chemicals and hazardous materials, and postal and shipping (CIPB 2002, p. 8).

Building upon the definition of critical infrastructure, this chapter establishes a conceptual framework for the book. By focusing on information infrastructure, the literature concerning its agglomeration and spatial characteristics is fused with work in complex networks that characterizes the structural topologies of information infrastructure networks. The theory of these two sets of literature establishes a unique view on the vulnerability of critical information infrastructure and the conceptual framework then addresses the impact and relevance to public policy. When examining information infrastructure, it is useful to first examine the economic forces behind it, and in turn the effect it has had on the economy to establish the first link in the conceptual framework.

THE ECONOMICS OF AGGLOMERATION

At the dawn of the information revolution, pundits proclaimed that the new economic landscape enabled by telecommunications would collapse time and space, making location irrelevant. In a search for lower cost areas to conduct business, economic activity would diffuse and cities would no longer serve as important agglomerations of activities, information, services and human resources (Sassen 1994). This was the view of globalization, through an information economy, implemented by a telecommunication revolution. While the world was globalizing and economic activity was dispersing, command and control was becoming increasingly vital to keep order and direction. In order to control a myriad of operations and information entailed in a global economy, business had to have central locations that were equipped with the communication and service infrastructure to facilitate these functions. Business was demanding an ever-increasing mass of facilities, services, physical infrastructure, and connectivity to compete in the globalized information economy. Only in the largest urban areas were these agglomerations of infrastructure and resources available for business to meet their new needs and functions. Far from being replaced, cities had evolved to a new order of importance, constituting the central nervous system of a globalized world. Large cities are now serving as the critical communication hubs for the information economy and the heart of critical infrastructure (Wheeler and O'Kelly 1999; Moss and Townsend 2000; Gorman and Malecki 2000; Malecki and Gorman 2001; Grubesic and O'Kelly 2002; Townsend 2001; Malecki and McIntee forthcoming).

WORLD CITIES THEORY

The concept of this new urban hierarchy of world/global cities is encapsulated in the ideas of the world cities system first proposed by Friedman (1986). The World Cities Theory gained acceptance and expanded, with new ideas being added to the paradigm, analyzing different aspects that contributed to the formation and dynamic evolution of world cities (Knox and Taylor 1995). One constant throughout research and writing about world cities system is the accumulation of telecommunications in metropolitan areas to link them together as command and control centers. It is the fundamental need of business to have a command and control center to communicate and direct, which has made global cities so important. According to world cities theory, the shift in the economy was correct, but the effect on the geography of space and place was not (Friedman 1986; Moss 1998; Sassen 1994). Cities did not vanish, but rose in primacy, developing into a new global urban hierarchy. A disproportionate agglomeration of ICT[1] (Townsend 2001), financial services (Warf 1995), and technology firms (Gorman 2002) in large metropolitan areas has been found in empirical research, delineating a distinct urban hierarchy of global cities (Beaverstock et al. 2000).

Telecommunications and IT have created a more profound spatial division of labor, allowing cities to be directly connected to branch and subsidiary locations in other regions (Atkinson 1998; Moss 1998; Pollard and Storper 1996). In the spatial division of labor, low-order economic activities have increasingly been exported to peripheral regions, but high-order economic activities increasingly concentrate in urban areas and especially global cities (Atkinson 1998; Howland 1993; Moss 1998; Pollard and Storper 1996; Wilson 1994). High-order activities have stayed in urban agglomerations to take advantage of the productivity benefits afforded by high density (Ciccione and Hall 1996). The same correlation between density and productivity can be extended to telecommunications and IT: the higher the telecommunications and information technology density, the more productive the agglomeration. This hypothetical result of applying Ciccione and Hall's findings would result in a cumulative causation cycle in which agglomeration increases productivity, inducing growth, which increases density, further increasing productivity. The linking of these agglomerations to their lower order activities requires telecommunication networks and infrastructure outside the city, connecting to the rest of the country and the globe. In order to understand the effects of economic agglomeration one must also appreciate the geography of the networks that connect them.

GEOGRAPHIC NETWORKS AND INFORMATION

The most prominent aspect of the telecommunications and information revolution is its ability, through phenomena like the Internet and satellite transmissions, to connect geographically separated locations (those that possess the appropriate technology levels). There has been an increased amount of attention paid to the spatial aspects of communication, but the foundations of the spatial analysis of networks have often been overlooked. Social science and specifically geography has a deep tradition in network and spatial analysis. Garrison (1968) did in-depth network analysis on the interstate highway system, analyzing the importance of nodes and links on location and development. This same vein of research was greatly expanded through Garrison's student Kansky (1963) and later with the work of Haggett and Chorley (1969). In addition, Nyusten and Dacey (1968) and later Taaffe and Gauthier (1973) expanded this research, applying network analysis to telephone networks and general infrastructure. This tradition of network analysis was picked up again by geographers to begin to analyze the Internet's network of networks.

SPATIAL ANALYSIS OF THE INTERNET

Specifically, examination of the backbone level of the Internet is an area that has enjoyed a significant level of analysis by geographers, planners, policy analysts, and regional economists (Wheeler and O'Kelly 1999; Moss and Townsend 2000; Gorman and Malecki 2000; Malecki and Gorman 2001; Grubesic and O'Kelly 2002; Townsend 2001). The findings of this research have been remarkably consistent. Backbone networks disproportionately agglomerate in the largest metropolitan areas, 'The critical importance of access to new technologies has highlighted the characteristic diffusion pattern: hierarchical – beginning first in large cities, where the largest markets are found, and then to progressively smaller places' (Malecki 2001, p. 10). These large markets cluster spatially into distinct groups like the Boston-Washington corridor and the LA-San Francisco complex that are fully interconnected to each other both by the telephone network (Langdale 1989) and the Internet backbones (Gorman and Malecki 2000; Moss and Townsend 2000; Wheeler and O'Kelly 1999). The result is that the spatial hierarchy of the United States is unique; the coasts are more connected to each other than they are to the interior of the country – the coasts are the core and the interior is the periphery (Gorman and Malecki 2000).

Statistical analysis has produced a very distinct profile for these highly connected hub cities. Leading cities in advanced telecommunication services have been found to have high concentrations of producer services, Financial Insurance and Real Estate (FIRE), low levels of manufacturing, high population, and high total personal income (Malecki 2001; Gorman and McIntee 2003; Leyshon 1996; Warf 1995). Further, these cities are predominantly world cities that serve as hubs for information services as well as serving as command and control functions for global firms (Knox and Taylor 1995; Friedman 1986; Townsend 2001; Malecki 2002).

The profile of these super-connected cities also influences the structure of the network at a micro level within the city. Longcore and Rees' (1996) examination of New York City's financial district demonstrates meaningful analysis of information technology and networks at a very local level. They found that in New York the historic Wall Street-centered financial district has had to disperse within the city to take advantage of buildings and real estate with sufficient built-in infrastructure and technology to handle the district's specialized role in the information economy. Without buildings lit by fiber optic connections, financial district firms were disconnected from the global economy.

Network analysis of the spatial networks of the Internet has only just begun to be investigated. Wheeler and O'Kelly (1999) examined the basic graph measures of several domestic US providers and analysis of city connectivity of the aggregated providers. Gorman and Malecki (2000) investigated the network topologies of several firms and how graph theoretic measures could be used to investigate competitive advantage and the nature of interconnection between networks. Later studies have looked at the structure of networks and city connectivity as a time series, finding large changes in bandwidth capacity (Malecki 2002; Townsend 2001), but little change in graph measures of connectivity (O'Kelly and Grubesic 2002). While connectivity indices have changed little over time the overall structure of the network has. Gorman and Kulkarni (2004) found that the aggregated US backbone network has been increasingly self-organized from 1997 to 2000, creating a more efficient, but more sparsely connected network. This research confirmed at a spatial level of analysis what was being found at a topological level in the study of complex networks. Several fields have generated work on complex networks, and the most relevant to the questions at hand will be covered next.

THEORETICAL UNDERPINNINGS FOR NETWORKS

Recently, the empirical findings regarding agglomeration of telecommunication infrastructure and services have found new theoretical support from a rather unlikely field, statistical physics. The study of the structural nature and complexity of networks has produced new insight into their general nature and development. Networks are ubiquitous in the everyday world, some obvious – the network of roads, the fiber networks connecting computers – and some not so obvious – the economic networks that enable globalization, molecular networks that keep human bodies functioning. Surprisingly these networks have many things in common, and understanding the complex and evolving nature of them has garnered an increasing amount of interest. All networks share a common construct of nodes connected together by links. The very simple concept of one location connecting to another quickly becomes an extremely complex phenomenon as the number of nodes and connections increases. Figuring out how these simple concepts evolve into incredibly complex and dynamic networks has produced a flurry of work in physics, computer science, molecular biology, sociology, and many other fields. The one aspect of networks commonly overlooked in this new field of inquiry is the geography of networks. The vast majority of research on complex networks revolves around abstract networks where geographic location is not considered, but as seen in the previous chapter, these networks have a profound impact on geography, which in turn influences economics and policy.

A REVIEW OF SMALL WORLDS AND COMPLEX NETWORK RESEARCH

The mathematical study of networks commonly falls under graph theory. Graph theory has been used to model a wide array of networks for empirical analysis, including transportation, communications, river basins and neural networks. Sometimes networks are less apparent, as with economics where companies are nodes and transactions between them are edges, or social networks where people are nodes and acquaintance is the edge (Arthur 1999; Wasserman and Faust 1994; Hayes 2000a, p.10). In physical networks like river basins, rivers are the links and the confluence of two rivers is the nodes, and these structures often form fractals (Barbera and Rosso 1989). Early graph theory analysis was confined to relatively small networks with a computationally manageable number of edges and nodes. This work included many applications from geographical analysis, especially with transportation networks. Kansky (1963), Berry and Marble (1968), Haggett and Chorley (1969), Nyusten and Dacey (1968), Taaffe and Gauthier (1973) as well as many others used the graph theoretical implications of transportation networks to help explain aspects of regional and national economies.

During roughly the same period, Erdös and Renyi (1960) were carrying out theoretical work focused on large complex graphs. Erdös and Renyi (ER) endeavored to use 'probabilistic methods' to solve problems in graph theory where a large number of nodes where involved (Albert and Barabási 2002, p. 54). Under this assumption they modeled large graphs utilizing algorithms where N nodes were randomly connected according to probability P, and found that when nodes were connected in this fashion they followed a Poisson distribution (Albert and Barabási 2002, p. 49). A more thorough review of random graphs can be found in the survey work of Bollobás (1985). Following Erdos and Renyi's findings their random models of network formation were widely used in several disciplines researching networks, the most topical to this research being Internet topology generators (Radoslavov et al. 2000).

The absence of detailed topological data for complex networks left random network models as the most widely used method of network simulation (Barabási 2001). As computing power increased and real world network data began to become available several empirical findings emerged. Three network characteristics frequently resulted from analysis of complex networks:

1. Short average path length
2. High level of clustering

3. Power law and exponential degree distributions
   (Albert and Barabási 2002, p. 48)

Short average path length indicates that the distance between any two nodes on the network is short; they can be reached in a few hops along edges. Clustering occurs when nodes locate topologically close to each other in cliques that are well connected to each other. Power law and exponential degree distributions will be described subsequently, since they require a more detailed introduction.

Watts and Strogatz (WS) (1998) formalized the concept of clustering for complex networks. Using several large data sets, they found that the real-world networks studied were not entirely random but instead displayed significant clustering at the local level. Further, they found that local clusters linked across the graph to each other forming 'small worlds'. To model this effect Watts and Strogatz (1998) took a regular lattice where all neighbors are connected to their two nearest neighbors and randomly rewired nodes in the lattice. These short cuts across the graph to different clusters of nodes introduced a level of efficiency[2] not predicted in the Erdos and Renyi model. The distribution was not Poisson as with the Erdos and Renyi model, but was bounded and decayed exponentially for large sets of nodes (Watts and Strogatz 1998). The work by Watts and Strogatz was not the first, though, to investigate the effects of rewiring: 'Fan R. K. Chung, in collaborations with Michael R. Garey of AT&T Laboratories and Béla Bolobás of the University of Memphis, studied various ways of adding edges to cyclic graphs. They found cases where the diameter is proportional to log n' (Hayes 2000b, p.106).

The finding of Watts and Strogatz spurred a flurry of work into understanding the attributes of complex networks, and new findings and discoveries quickly followed. Two parallel studies by Albert, Jeong, and Barabási (1999) of Notre Dame, and Huberman and Adamic (1999) at Xerox Parc found that when one looks at the World Wide Web as a graph (web pages are nodes and hyperlinks connecting them are edges) it followed not a Poisson or exponential distribution, but a power law distribution.

A power law is a significantly different finding from either the expected exponential or Poisson distribution. In a power law distribution there is an abundance of nodes with only a few links, and a small but significant minority that have a very large number of links (Barabási 2002). It should be noted that this is a distinct difference from both the ER and WS models; the probability of finding a highly connected node in the ER and WS models decreases exponentially, thus, 'nodes with high connectivity are practically absent' (Barabási and Albert 1999, p. 510). The reason, according to Barabási and Albert (1999), was that their model added another perspective to complex networks, incorporating network growth; the number of nodes does not stay constant as in the WS and ER models. The Barabási and Albert models added growth over time and the idea that new nodes attach preferentially to already well-connected nodes in the network.

Barabási and Albert (1999) formalized this idea in 'Emergence of scaling in random networks'. They stated that in a complex network like the World Wide Web, the probability $P(k)$ that a node in the network interacts with k other nodes decays as a power law following $P(k) \sim k^{-\gamma}$ where the power law exponent is equal to 3 (see Figure 4.1 for a graphic representation of the function).

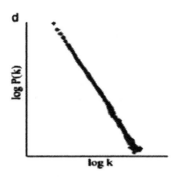

Source: Barabási, 2001.

Figure 4.1   Sample power law distribution

When studying real-world scale-free networks, empirical results have ranged from 2.1 to 4 (Barabási and Albert 1999). While the model set up by Barabási and Albert produces an exponent of 3, they demonstrate how the model can be altered to produce results other than 3 for different network conditions. The Barabási-Albert (BA) model is based on three mechanisms that drive the evolution of graph structures over time to produce power law relationships:

1. Incremental growth – Incremental growth follows from the observation that most networks develop over time by adding new nodes and new links to existing graph structure.
2. Preferential connectivity – Preferential connectivity expresses the frequently encountered phenomenon that there is higher probability for a new or existing node to connect or reconnect to a node that already

has a large number of links (i.e. high node degree) than there is to (re)connect to a low degree node.

3. Re-wiring – Re-wiring allows for some additional flexibility in the formation of networks by removing links connected to certain nodes and replacing them with new links in a way that effectively amounts to a local type of re-shuffling connection based of preferential attachment. (Chen et al. 2001, p.5)

The difference between the random model of Erdös and Renyi and the model described by Barabási and Albert becomes clearer when visualized. Figure 4.2 illustrates the structural difference between a random Erdös and Renyi network model and a scale-free network model.

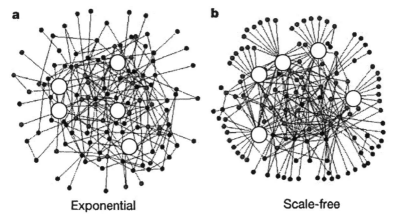

Exponential   Scale-free

Source: Barabási 2001, p.1.

Figure 4.2   *The difference between random exponential networks and scale-free networks*

The high level of clustering is evident on the node. For the model in Figure 4.2, more than 60 percent of nodes (small gray and black) can be reached from the five most-connected nodes (large white) in the scale-free network, compared with only 27 percent in the random network. This demonstrates the key role that hubs play in the scale-free network. Both networks contain the 130 nodes and 430 links (Barabási 2001, p.1)

Figure 4.2 makes clear the hubbing effect caused by the preferential attachment mechanism in scale-free networks; 60 percent of the nodes are directly connected to the top five hubs.

A difficult question to find an answer for in the literature revolves around the classification of a small world and a scale-free network. As stated earlier, Albert and Barabási (2002) see small worlds and scale-free networks as explanations for two different phenomena occurring in complex networks. The WS small world model explains clustering, and the scale-free model explains power law degree distributions (Albert and Barabási 2002, p.49). There have, though, been other opinions on how small world and scale-free networks should be classified. Amaral et al. (2000) posits that scale-free networks are a sub class of small world networks, and that there are three classes of small world networks:

1. Scale-free networks, characterized by a node connectivity distribution that decays as a power law.
2. Broad-scale networks, characterized by a connectivity distribution that has a power law regime followed by a sharp cut-off.
3. Single-scale networks, characterized by a connectivity distribution with a fast decaying tail.
   (Amaral et al. 2000, p.11149)

Delineating which of the three classes a network might fall under is determined through an examination of their rank order connectivity distributions and a log-log plot. Fitting a line to this distribution will indicate how close the network's connectivity distribution comes to a power law distribution indicative of a scale-free network. As such there is not a straightforward statistical test that determines the type or class of a real world network outside the shape of its connectivity distribution. Examining a network's diameter and clustering coefficients will establish whether or not it is small world, but its class of 'small world' is a more opinionated matter. An exact delineation of where small world and scale-free networks diverge is still somewhat unclear in the literature, but the area of study is still evolving. It can be concluded that the two are inter-related and that generally speaking, scale-free networks exhibit the short average path length of small world networks, but not all small world networks exhibit the power law distribution of scale-free networks.

An important caveat to the scale-free network concept should be introduced at this point. The scale-free theory proposed by Barabási and Albert (1999) is a topology generator that replicates the connectivity distribution seen in many real world networks. Since their connectivity distributions are a power law and hence are scale-free, they are often called scale-free networks. However, this does not mean these real world network's topologies are the same as those produced by a scale-free topology generator. One of the unresolved questions posed by Barabási and Albert's research is whether the topology of their generator matches the topology of real world networks. Just because the generator produces a power law distribution does not necessarily mean that it also replicates the topology of a real network. There are a range of network topologies that could result in a scale-free power distribution of network connectivity. Several researchers have specifically investigated whether scale-free topology generators match real world topologies. In regards to information infrastructure, two studies in particular stand out: Willinger's (2002) study on WWW network topologies and Alderson et al.'s (2003) study of Internet topologies. The Willinger study found that in a study of WWW topology, preferential attachment did not follow the age of vertex as proposed by the original BA model, and there was no correlation between the age of web page and its connectivity. The Alderson et al. (2003) study found that the inclusion of economic trade-offs and technical constraints under the framework of highly optimized tolerance did a better job of replicating real world Internet topologies than the scale-free BA model.

Fitness models have been used to explain variations and discrepancies from the scale-free outcome (Bianconi and Barabási 2001). In the standard scale-free model, nodes attain preferential attachment by the fact they were the first nodes in the networks, in essence capturing the idea of 'first mover advantage'. Using a fitness model, 'the probability $?_i$ that a new node connects one of its m links to a node i already present in the network depends on the number of links k_i and on the fitness n_i of node i' (Bianconi and Barabási 2001 p. 5632), such that:

$$\prod_i = \frac{n_i k_i}{\sum_\ell n_\ell k_\ell} \qquad (4.1)$$

Bianconi and Barabási (2001) extend this idea further, illustrating that the dynamical properties of networks can be predicted 'within the framework of equilibria quantum gases' (p.5632), specifically as a Bose-Einstein condensation. Utilizing this technique, 'first-mover-advantage', 'fit-get-rich', and 'winner-takes-all' phenomena are illustrated. The 'winner-takes-all' outcome is of particular interest since one node ends up with all or the vast majority of connections. This outcome has parallels to many technology markets where one vendor or company ends up with the majority of the market share, such as personal computer operating systems.

The implications of this complex networks research affect a number of disciplines as varied as genetics, economics, molecular physics and sociology. One of the surprising findings was that not only did the World Wide Web fall into a scale-free connectivity distribution, so did the Internet. The Faloutsos brothers (Faloutsos et al. 1999) found that the Internet followed power laws at both the router level and autonomous system (AS) level. The router level entails the fiber optic lines (edges) and the routers (nodes) that direct traffic on the Internet, and the AS level entail networks (AT&T, UUNet, C&W, and so on) as nodes, and their interconnection as edges. This meant that the physical fabric of the Internet and the business interconnections of the networks that comprise the Internet both qualified as scale-free connectivity distributions. Before these discoveries, the Internet had been modeled as a distinct hierarchy or random network. The new finding had many implications throughout the field of computer science. The scale-free theory and BA model have not been without debate. Several arguments have been made stating that the BA model is too simplistic for the Internet, and that additional corollaries need to be made (Chen et al. 2001). The re-wiring principle was one of Albert and Barabási's (2000) responses to these criticisms. Tests of network generators based on power laws have been found to produce better models, and efforts are being made to base new Internet protocols on these discoveries (Tangmunarunkit et al. 2002; Radoslavov et al. 2000). The area is still hotly debated regarding topology generation, but the finding of scale-free power law distributions in the Internet has persisted. While these discoveries have paved the way for advancements in several fields, the question of the geography and location of these networks remains to be addressed.

NETWORK EVOLUTION

Analyzing spatial networks adds an additional variable to the problem, which increases the complexity of the issue. For one, networks can be planar or non-planar[3]. While this is not unique to spatial networks it does cause unique constraints. The majority of spatial networks that are based on Euclidean distance are planar. For instance, in a road network, when two streets cross, generally speaking, you have an intersection. The number of edges that can be connected to a single node is limited by the physical space available to connect them. This fact makes the large number of connections needed for a power law distribution quite difficult to obtain. Even in non-planar spatial networks such as airline networks, the number of connections is limited by the space available at the airport; 'such constraints may be the controlling factor for the emergence of scale-free networks' (Amaral et al. 2000, p.11149).

It should be noted that Amaral et al. (2000) did find that the airline network was a small world because of its small average path length, and other transportation networks such as the Boston subway have also been found to be small worlds (Latora and Marchiori 2002). It would seem that physical constraints prevent the formation of scale-free networks in traditional transport networks, but is this true when one examines the transportation networks of an information economy. The information economy in part depends on fiber optic lines to transport digital goods and services. Fiber optic networks have a physical location and structure, and can be analyzed as such.

Many have considered the dearth of attention to location and geography to result because they are too complicated to fit into current network models (Batty 2001). Some initial work by Yook et al. (2001) has examined the role of linear distance in complex networks. This work was extended at the global level when the Internet router network was examined, finding that the physical layout of nodes form a fractal set, determined by population density patterns around the globe (Yook et al. 2001). A similar study at Boston University found the same effect when population was controlled for with the per capita GDP of regions (Lakhina et al. 2002). Barthelemy (2003) found that in spatial networks with scale-free properties, long distance links connect predominantly to hubs. Further, if the total length in a network is fixed, the optimal network which minimizes both the total length and the diameter lies in between the scale-free and spatial networks (Barthelemy 2003). Large complex networks, like the Internet, pose problems beyond the spatial and computational problems outlined above.

PROTECTING COMPLEX NETWORKS

The Internet is also an amalgam of thousands of interconnected networks. Some of these networks are vast global networks like Worldcom (MCI) or Cable & Wireless, while others are small local networks like a university. The individual networks that compose the Internet are commonly called autonomous systems (AS) and number roughly 12,000 active ASs, with 22,000 assigned and roughly 65,000 ASs possible (based on a 16-bit number) (Gao 2001). The task of trying to provide a minimum level of security for all these networks is a daunting effort, but one that has been increasingly highlighted as an area of importance for national security (CIPB 2002, NRC 2002b, NSTAC 2002). Innovative approaches are called for to tackle a problem of such a large scale and increasingly global nature. Recently, researchers in the many fields have begun work concerning the fundamental structure of complex interaction of the networks that comprise the Internet (Faloutsos et al. 1999, Tangmunarunkit et al. 2002, Lakhina et al. 2002, Yook et al. 2001). Much of the work has revolved around the finding that the Internet at the AS and router level forms a scale-free network (Faloutsos et al. 1999, Albert and Barabási 2002). An understanding of the mechanics underlying the growth and evolution of the

Internet provides a new perspective for the role policy can play in helping foster a more secure Internet. The work done on complex networks has laid the groundwork for many findings on the vulnerability of information infrastructure, especially the Internet. In order to understand the application of this research it is necessary to first provide a brief survey of how the Internet operates, to give appropriate context.

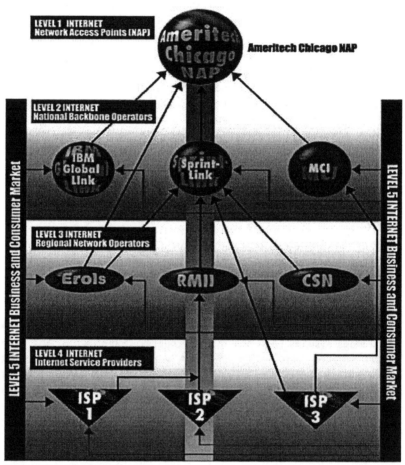

Source: Boardwatch 1998.

Figure 4.3   Network levels diagram

INTERNET STRUCTURE

The Internet, despite its depiction by Internet engineers as an amorphous cloud (Kostas et al. 1998; Rodriguez-Moral 1997; Cavanaugh 1998), has a definite physical structure and hierarchy. In the simplest sense, the Internet is a network – or, more accurately, a network of networks. The Internet is composed of a wide variety of small, medium and large networks that all interconnect to different degrees to give the seamless impression of one big machine. Since the Internet is composed of such a wide range of different networks, owners, operators and technologies, it relies on a structured hierarchy and protocol to operate.

This hierarchy of network interconnectedness fundamentally divides into five levels, illustrated in Figure 4.3. The first layer consists of the network access points, designated NAPs. NAPs are hub points where networks can exchange data between each other. A user whose Internet service is provided through Sprint can send an email to a friend who is connected through AT&T from Sprint's proprietary network to AT&T's proprietary network. The email (data) must be transferred between networks, and this is done at NAPs or other transfer points in a process called peering.

Level two is comprised of national backbone providers. National backbone providers make available transit services for data between city nodes across the United States and the world. If the Sprint user, above, sends an email from his computer in New York to a friend's computer in Washington, DC, the email would traverse a Sprint backbone connecting these two cities. It is important to note that not all cities are directly connected, or perhaps are not connected at all, by transit backbones.

Regional network providers comprise the third level of connection in the hierarchy. If the recipient of the Sprint email in the Washington, DC area actually lives in Springfield, VA, in order to reach the Springfield region south of DC, the email must 'hop' onto a regional network, such as Erols[4], in order to access the many suburbs of northern Virginia. National backbones do not service all cities, just those large enough to create a market opportunity for firms.

Following the hierarchy, the Internet Service Provider (ISP) is the fourth level of service. The email from New York has filtered down to the regional network, but our end-user has his personal Internet and email connection through Springfield Net, a local ISP. The email then hops off the Erols regional network onto Springfield Net, and is delivered through a dial-up analog modem to the end-user's house, the fifth level of the hierarchy.

Each of the networks in the four levels is called an autonomous system, or AS. Autonomous system means that each operates independently of the other and sets its own policies and network structure. It is only through peering that these networks become interconnected to form the core of the Internet. In the words of Christian Huitema, the President of the Internet Architecture Board:

> ASs provide natural aggregates for 'high-level' [network] maps, where nodes would not be routers but the ASs themselves [their city nodes], and the only links we consider will be those linking ASs. [Further] one may want to consider only those ASs that perform 'transit' services. There will be thousands of stub or multi-homed ASs, but they will be at the periphery of the network. (Huitema 1995, p.227)

As Huitema points out, ASs can also be divided into transit ASs and two other categories as well:

- Stub AS - It is connected to only one other AS. For routing purposes it is treated as part of the parent AS.
- Multihomed AS - It is connected to more than one other AS, but does not allow transit traffic. Internally generated traffic can be routed to any of the connected ASs. It is used in large corporate networks that have a number of Internet connections, but do not want to carry traffic for others.
- Transit AS - It is connected to more than one other AS and it can be used to carry transit traffic between other ASs. (Magoni and Pansiot 2001)

Where these transit backbones are located and how they are connected have become increasingly important issues as technology develops. Wired and wireless infrastructures are increasingly tethered to a fiber optic (transit) backbone for connectivity into the domestic and global network (Gorman and McIntee 2003). Fiber optic cable is quickly replacing analog and digital, microwave and satellite for point-to-point, long-haul backbone telecommunications service. Satellite and microwave systems cannot compete economically or practically with these new terrestrial and undersea fiber systems.

WHEN INTERNET INFRASTRUCTURE IS ATTACKED

On Saturday 15 January, 2003 at 5:30a.m., the SQL Slammer worm emerged from somewhere in East Asia and propagated around the globe, doubling every 8.5 seconds and infecting 90 percent of vulnerable machines in under 10 minutes (Moore et al. 2003). While the SQL Slammer did not carry a malicious payload, the sheer amount of traffic it produced swamped networks causing 13,000 Bank of America ATMs to become disconnected, airline flights to be canceled, and elections and 911 services to be disrupted. The spread of the SQL slammer worm was a warning of not only the speed and scope of malicious worms but the level of interdependency of the Internet with other critical infrastructures (banking and finance, transportation, medical, public safety and governance). The speed of the worm is all the more confounding when the spread and the complexity of infrastructure it traversed is considered.

ERROR AND ATTACK TOLERANCE OF COMPLEX NETWORKS

Scale-free networks have many implications, but a far-reaching consequence of their unique structure is that they are very fault tolerant but also susceptible to attack (Albert et al. 2000). Specifically, a scale-free network model remains connected when up to 80 percent of nodes are randomly removed from the network, but when the most-connected nodes are removed, the average path length of the network increases rapidly, doubling its original value when the top 5 percent of nodes are removed (Albert et al. 2000). In short, targeting the most-connected nodes can cause significant damage to a scale-free network, making them highly susceptible to a coordinated and targeted attack. Further, these numbers and findings were highly similar when real world networks were tested, including the Internet at the autonomous system level and the WWW; when the most-connected networks and web pages were attacked, the network rapidly failed. Albert et al.'s work was complemented by the analysis of Callaway et al. (2000) modeling network robustness and fragility as a percolation, and by Cohen et al. (2001) using related methodologies. Preliminary analyses of these models on spatial network data have shown similar results when cities are the nodes and fiber connections between them are the links. Utilizing a model of node connectivity and path availability Grubesic et al. (2003) find that the disconnection of a major hub city can cause the disconnection of peripheral cities from the network. Spatial analysis of network failure has also been done for airline networks finding similar results for the Indian airline network (Cliff et al. 1979).

THE SPREAD OF MALICIOUS ATTACKS IN COMPLEX NETWORKS

The scale-free structure of the Internet also has implications for how malicious attacks like worms and viruses are propagated throughout the network. Viruses and worms are not trivial computer nuisances, but high-cost problems:

> By the end of August, the cost of virus attacks in 2001 totaled nearly $10.7 billion, according to researchers at Computer Economics. In previous years, computer viruses have done quite a bit of financial damage, the group says. During 2000, virus attacks cost an estimated $17.1 billion, with the Love Bug and its 50 variants doing about $8.7 billion worth of harm. And in 1999, the estimated damage was reported to be $12.1 billion...Code Red accounted for $2.6 billion in damage - $1.5 billion in lost productivity and $1.1 billion in clean-up costs (Lawyer 2003).

The high cost of virus and worm attacks on the Internet and connected businesses highlights the importance of understanding how these attacks spread and what steps might be taken to mitigate them. The scale-free and power law nature of the Internet illustrated by Barabási (2002) and Faloutsos et al. (1999) point to a methodological framework for examining this problem. Analysis of epidemics in scale-free networks first reported by Pastor-Satorras and Vespignani (2001) found that a wide range of scale-free networks did not have an epidemic threshold. The lack of an epidemic threshold[5] meant that infections would persist and spread irrespective of the rate of the infections; however, the outcome is dependent on the particular structure and topology of networks. This, in theory, could explain why viruses are rarely eradicated from the Internet and tend to spread quickly even when injected from peripheral places. Pastor-Satorras and Vespignani (2002) extended this work, examining immunization of complex networks including an empirical test of the Internet at the AS level. In their test, a SIS (susceptible-infected-susceptible) model was implemented, where half of the nodes in the network were infected and then nodes were immunized, and the effect on infection rates recorded. They found that targeted immunizations performed significantly better than uniform immunization strategies.

Dezso and Barabási (2002) directly address the prospects of stopping such viruses, finding that traditional methods did not succeed in slowing spread rates or eradicating viruses. The authors instead found that selectively protecting the most-connected nodes in the network could restore an epidemic threshold and 'potentially eradicate a virus' (p.1). The study also shows that a policy approach based on a 'protect the hubs' strategy is cost effective, in that it expends resources on only a few targeted nodes (Dezso and Barabási 2002, p.3). The Dezso and Barabási (2002) study, based on theoretical models instead of empirical data, leaves some question of how effective their strategy would be with actual networks. A recent study by Newman et al. (2002) studied a 16,881-user email network to determine how viruses would spread across the network. While the structure of the network was not the power law distribution seen in the theoretical scale-free models discussed above, the network's exponential distribution still reacted similarly to the predicted models. Protecting the most connected email users (in the form of anti-virus software or other measures) in the network had significantly better results than randomly protecting users across the network.

VULNERABILITY OF SPATIAL NETWORKS

Preliminary analyses of the vulnerability of spatial network data have shown similar results to the complex network literature, when cities are the nodes and fiber connections between them are the links. When the most connected cities are targeted for failure, the network diameter increases dramatically and fails catastrophically with 10 percent of the most connected nodes removed (Gorman and Kulkarni, 2004). Utilizing a different model of node connectivity and path availability, Grubesic et al. (2003) found that the disconnection of a major hub city can cause the disconnection of peripheral cities from the network. Spatial analysis of network failure has also been done for airline networks, finding similar results for the Indian airline network (Cliff et al. 1979). These findings point to the need for further investigation of spatial networks and vulnerability to attack.

SHORTCOMINGS

The collective work on the nature of complex networks and the spread of worms or viruses points to a possible fruitful approach for policies that could help provide greater cybersecurity. Questions, though, still remain as to how a 'protect the hubs' strategy would play out across the Internet as a whole, and what level of protection would be needed to gain the maximum level of security with the minimal level of investment. Is there a distinctive phase transition where protecting a certain percentage of nodes results in a big jump in overall network security? Further, considering the global nature of the Internet can any one country implement policies that would affect enough of the network to make an appreciable impact on global network security.

PUBLIC POLICY AND CYBERSECURITY

A negative externality of a scale-free network structure is security. The literature of complex networks shows that certain network formations, like scale-free networks, are very vulnerable to targeted attacks. This has direct implications for critical infrastructure protection, which largely revolves around the protection of national networks. Hunker (2002) states that the policies required for critical infrastructure are intrinsically tied to understanding the complexity and interdependencies of the nation's networks. Part of this understanding is the role of geography, and what role it plays in the complexity of network interdependency and the policy implications (Rinaldi et al. 2001). If the properties that make complex networks susceptible to attack also manifest themselves at a geographic level this will be an area of research interest with many policy implications. Already cybersecurity and critical infrastructure have attracted considerable policy attention. Most notable have been the Federal Reserve, the Securities and Exchange Commission (SEC), the Office of the Comptroller of the Currency (OCC), and the State of New York Banking Department's issuance of the 'Draft Interagency White Paper on Sound Practices to Strengthen the Resilience of the US Financial System' and the White House Critical Infrastructure Protection Board's February 2003 release of 'The National Strategy to Secure Cyberspace'.

'The National Strategy to Secure Cyberspace' has received criticism from several venues, specifically concerning the lack of three features:

1. An assessment of the threat and the cost of inaction
2. A link between the policy objectives and incentives
3. The strategy rejects regulation, government standards, and use of liability laws in addressing the cybersecurity issue (Berkowitz and Hahn 2003, p.6)

It is argued that the lack of these three features prevents any kind of cost-benefit analysis from being done. Further, it is argued that without a cost-benefit analysis there is no threshold for determining which of the activities and plans in the strategy are worth investing in or pursuing (Berkowitz and Hahn 2003, p.6). Without an analysis of the range of policy options the best strategy cannot be determined. Hunker (2002) deals specifically with the range of public policy interventions that could deal with global information infrastructure security. Specifically he outlines:

1. Market forces
2. Regulation
3. Tort liability and contracts
4. Voluntary standards and best practices
5. Insurance
6. Public disclosure
7. Reputation/ratings
8. Procurement

Regarding these options, Hunker also states that the large sunk cost in information infrastructure by network providers makes them unwilling to invest in implementing cybersecurity measures. Further, network providers' security is dependent on the security of all other interconnected networks, resulting in a prisoner's dilemma situation (Kunreuther et al. 2002). The National Strategy argues that policy interventions like regulation, standards, and liability would impede innovation and hamper international competitiveness. The plan's strategy and countervailing arguments remain to be empirically tested.

NOTES

1. Information and communication technologies
2. Efficiency in this case refers to the network characteristic of a large number of nodes having a low diameter
3. Planar networks form nodes whenever two edges cross, whereas non-planar networks can have edges that cross without forming nodes
4. While the Boardwatch diagram is still architecturally correct, the business landscape has changed. Erols was purchased by Starpower and no longer exists today, but the technical explanation of interconnection is still valid.
5. The epidemic threshold is the point at which the percentage of unvaccinated people is high enough to risk an epidemic

5. The Vulnerability of Networks and the Resurrection of Distance

One of the most important and often overlooked aspects of critical infrastructure is where it is located. Many times critical infrastructures are investigated with models to make the complexity of networks manageable. While this approach yields many useful insights, the inclusion of the geography of critical infrastructure is vital for dealing with the issue of how to protect it and determining 'where' it is vulnerable. This chapter includes geography in the analysis of critical information infrastructure. In a broad perspective spatial (or geographic) variables are incorporated into the complex network theory discussed previously. These variables will be incorporated into algorithms to ascertain the criticality of nodes in the tested network. Once spatial variables have been incorporated, the vulnerability of the networks to failures is simulated. The analysis will provide insight into which algorithm does the best job in determining what is most critical in a network and if incorporating spatial variables improves results. Further, the testing examines how increased cooperation and interconnection in networks affects resiliency.

Once the experiment has been carried out, a discussion of how logical networks can be analyzed in conjunction with physical fiber networks is attempted. While the approach outlined in the first experiment works well for logical networks it does not work well for analysis of physical (geographic) fiber networks, especially when more than one provider is involved along a common right of way. In order to analyze the vulnerabilities of physical fiber, a new heat-mapping tool is presented. The heat-mapping tool defines areas where there is a high density of fiber lines but a small amount of diversity. This tool is then used to test whether a GIS based grid density analysis of physical fiber networks will illustrate areas of high vulnerability in areas with low population. First, though, the vulnerability and criticality of information infrastructure is examined.

METHODOLOGY

In order to test the susceptibility of the spatial US information infrastructure to attack, multiple approaches were developed building upon prior studies and literature. Several studies have noted that the removal of critical nodes caused a rapid degradation of the network. Generally, these nodes are determined to be critical based on their level of connectivity, often referred to as an accessibility index in spatial network analysis. The first methodological step of this study is to determine which nodes are most critical and what is the best way to identify them. The next step is to test the set of nodal hierarchies and to see which ranking method has the greatest impact on the network when nodes are targeted for failure and what the ripple effect of their removal is. Next, an attempt is made to develop an analysis that allows the modeling of physical fiber networks with logical (operational) networks. This approach will allow some understanding of the impact that a cut or a failure in the physical network will have on the logical network. Finally, analysis of physical fiber that is not amenable to graph theoretical techniques is undertaken with the use of a vulnerability heat-mapping tool. Data is analyzed for each step of the methodology and conclusions drawn. First, though, the methodology for identifying critical nodes in a network is presented.

METHODS FOR DEVELOPING NODAL HIERARCHIES

One of the most important tasks in critical infrastructure is deciding what is critical. When a critical infrastructure is a network, one approach is to analyze which nodes are most critical. This can be accomplished by creating nodal hierarchies, which rank nodes from most critical to least critical. There are many methods for establishing nodal hierarchies within a network, and classical spatial network analysis has some standard approaches. The most common of these is the accessibility index:

$$A_i = \sum_{i=1}^{n} d_{ij} \qquad (5.1)$$

The accessibility index provides the number of connections to a node; in the case of this study each MSA is considered to be a node. Another derivation of the accessibility index is to look at not only the binary connectivity of a node, but also the capacity of those links:

$$A_i' = \sum_{i=1}^{n} c_{ij} \qquad (5.2)$$

$c = capacity\ of\ the\ link$

While both of these approaches to nodal hierarchies provide useful insight into connectivity and criticality of nodes, there are some drawbacks. These nodal hierarchies are based on some fundamental assumptions:

1. There are a certain number of discrete classes of settlements.
2. The number of settlements in each size class increases down the hierarchy.
3. There is some characteristic spacing between nearest neighbors at any particular level. (Lowe and Moryadas 1975)

The drawback of this approach is that it is based on a spatial-hierarchical structuring of an idealized Loschian[1] (Losch 1954) landscape (Haggett 1969). In a Loschian landscape nodes will connect and goods will flow based on proximity with larger places connecting to each other through intervening smaller places (Haggett 1969). This approach is based on a planar network, where the intersection of any two links always results in a node. Information networks, though, are non-planar constructs where two distant places can be directly connected without intervening nodes being intersected. As a result, traditional methods of determining nodal hierarchies may not be appropriate.

Recent research into complex networks has found that information networks often form small world or scale-free networks. The general attribute of these formations is that there are formations of local clusters that are interconnected through global connections. This creates a highly efficient and sparsely connected network. Vulnerability studies have focused on identifying the global connections in these systems and then targeting them for failure or attack (Albert et al. 2000, Cohen et al. 2001, Callaway et al. 2000). These studies all found that removing the global connectors in the network led to catastrophic failure. This leaves the question of how global connectors should be identified in a spatial network. Further, how should local clustering and global connections be determined?

One nodal hierarchy approach is to use regions to define what is global and what is local (Gorman and Kulkarni 2004). In this approach the United States is divided into the four census regions (South, West, Midwest, Northeast) and each city in the information infrastructure matrix is assigned to a census region. For each city the number of local links to other cities in the same census region is totaled along with the number of global links connecting to cities in other census regions. From this data the following approach is developed to identify cities that act as the super connected cities that provide the key global connections in the network:

Consider a large network of n nodes, spanning an area A consisting of m regions, with a variable number of nodes inside each region that have a variable number of connections from each region to other regions. For a region r with p number of nodes, a $p \times p$ contiguity matrix represents connections between these nodes. Then, one could construct a contiguity or adjacency matrix for the entire network of m regions, as a block diagonal matrix, where matrices along the main diagonal refer to the contiguity matrices for each of the regions, while interregional connections are represented as the off-block-diagonal elements. Let M denote such a matrix.

If a node i in region r is connected to another node j in the same region, then that connection is considered to be a local link and is denoted:

$$q_{i(r)j(r)} \tag{5.3}$$

On the other hand if node i in region r is connected to node k in region s then that connection is considered to be a global connection and is denoted:

$$g_{i(r)k(s)} \tag{5.4}$$

Thus, in theory, one may associate with each node $i(r)$, a global connectivity index as a ratio between its global and local connections, weighted by the total number of global and local connections for the entire network.

The total number of global connections G is computed from the elements of the block upper triangular matrix of M, of m regions, each with a variable number of nodes:

$$\tag{5.5}$$

$$G = \sum_{i(1)}^{m} \sum_{s>1} \sum_{k(s)} g_{i(1)k(s)} + \sum_{i(2)}^{m} \sum_{s>2} \sum_{k(s)} g_{i(2)k(s)} + \ldots + \sum_{i(m-1)}^{m} \sum_{s>m-1} \sum_{k(s)} g_{i(m-1)k(s)}$$

Note that, since m is the last region in the block diagonal matrix, its global connections have already been computed in the previous m-1 blocks.

The total number of local connections L is a sum over all the local connections over m regions and is given by:

$$L = \sum_{i(1)} \sum_{j(1)>i(1)} q_{i(1)j(1)} + \sum_{i(2)} \sum_{j(2)>i(2)} q_{i(2)j(2)} + \ldots + \sum_{i(m)} \sum_{j(m)>i(m)} q_{i(m)j(m)} \tag{5.6}$$

Then the global connectivity index for a node i in region r is given by:

$$C_{i(r)} = \left(\frac{\sum\limits_{s \neq r}^{m} \sum\limits_{k(s)} g_{i(r)k(s)}}{1 + \sum\limits_{j(r), j \neq i} q_{i(r)j(r)}} \right) \times (G + L) \qquad (5.7)$$

The numeral of 1 in the denominator indicates a self-loop of a node. The ratio of global links to local links provides an indicator of how well the city acts as a global connector in the network, and the weighting of the scores by the total number of links balances the measure with the overall connectivity of the node.

This approach has several drawbacks, the most obvious being a border effect. Those nodes located close to a border can have a very short link that crosses to another census region, artificially inflating the number of global connections. An alternative approach is to determine what is a global link and what is a local one by using the Euclidean length of the link, a distance-based small world. Any link over x miles is considered global and anything under x miles is considered local. This approach would yield the following equation:

$$\left(\frac{\sum\limits_{j} g_{ij} > D}{1 + \sum\limits_{j} l_{ij} \leq D} \right) \left(\sum\limits_{j} g_{ij} + \sum\limits_{j} l_{ij} \right) \qquad (5.8)$$

The problem lies in determining what the distance should be for the cut-off between what is considered global or local. To gain some perspective on this problem, the equation is automated, and a series of alternative distances for D is selected and used to simulate global/local ratios:

$$\text{Where } \quad D \in [100, 200, 300...2700] \qquad (5.9)$$

The simulations produced the graph presented in Figure 5.1, where the x-axis shows the increments of the global/local ratio produced by different values of D, and the y-axis shows the percentage of nodes with a global to local ratio greater than one. Figure 5.1 shows a sharp shift at about 300 miles and a second shift at about 700 miles.

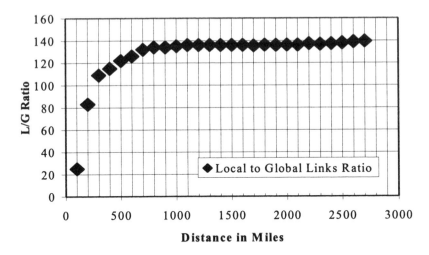

Figure 5.1   Local to global links ratio by distance

To find the exact point of inflection, the rate of change in the global to local ratio was calculated, as illustrated in Figure 5.2.

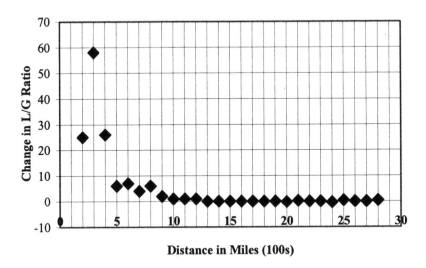

Figure 5.2   Rate of change of local to global link ratio

The rate of change graph clearly points to 300 miles as being the primary point of inflection. Under such an assumption all links shorter than 300 miles are considered local, and all links over 300 miles are considered global. Interestingly 300 miles is very close to the mean distance of all links in the matrix, 308.6 miles. Further, the average length of private leased lines (a different set of data) in the United States is 300 miles (Coffman and Odlyzko 1998). The recurring nature of 300 miles could point to a common spatial structure in the United States for communication networks. This is an area that merits further investigation and possible cross-country comparisons.

Another hierarchy was developed based on the distance small world approach, which examined the number of global connections a node has, and ranked the nodes based on that count. The equation would then be:

$$\sum_j g_{ij} > D \tag{5.10}$$

This ranking would provide an indicator of how many long-haul global connections a city has dictated by connections longer than D, which is 300 miles in this case. The hypothesis is that the more global connections, the greater the impact the loss of the node will have in connecting various clusters across the network. A final approach considered for this study is to identify relay nodes and what effect they are having on the survivability of the network. Relay nodes are typically defined as locations that are neither the ultimate origin nor destination of an interaction across a network.

The primary purpose of a relay node is to receive flows in order to transmit them to another node with minimum delay and cost (Lowe and Moryadas 1975). On information networks like the Internet the definition of a relay node is more fluid. Nodes constantly shift from being origin, destination, or relay nodes. This requires sorting which nodes are disproportionately used as relay nodes. Nodes that act as structural links to relay information to large markets could serve as critical junctures. To sort out which nodes are disproportionately acting as relay nodes, the following approach was developed:

$$\frac{\sum_{i=1}^{n} c_{ij}}{\sum_{i=1}^{n} b_{ij}} \tag{5.11}$$

where c_{ij} = capacity and b_{ij} = business demand

This approach provides a rough indicator of how much built capacity exceeds the consumption of capacity dictated by demand, by taking a ratio of capacity to a node by the demand for that capacity. It is assumed that nodes with an aggregate disproportionate amount of excess capacity are using it to relay information to other destination nodes. The hypothesis for a relay node hierarchy is that these nodes are structurally important in linking up large destination nodes, and without them connection would be severely affected. The result of applying these ranking algorithms is covered once the data and measurement methodologies are covered.

DATA

With a series of nodal ranking approaches designed, a data set is needed to which to apply them. For this study a data set of aggregated IP network providers from the year 2000 is used, comprising a matrix of 147 metropolitan statistical areas and the IP bandwidth available between each one (Malecki 2002). It should be noted that the accuracy of the data is imperfect. IP network providers' maps often advertise more capacity than is currently in operation, and future routes are often shown as current routes. With this shortcoming in mind, the data does however provide an adequate test base to compare algorithms and examine rough rankings. Further, the aggregation of this data set assumes that all networks interconnect with all other networks in every city they collocate in. This is far from the case in reality, but provides a best-case scenario for testing purposes. From this capacity matrix, a binary connectivity and Euclidean distance matrix are constructed. Finally business demand for the relay node hierarchy was calculated from FCC figures tabulated by Telegeography (2002). The FCC data though is only used to calculate the relay node algorithm and does not add to the structure of the network the simulations are run on.

In order to test the effect of these nodal hierarchies on the US IP Network outlined above, each rank-order is subjected to two simulations. In the first simulation each node is successively removed according to its rank and the diameter of the network is measured for each removal. The diameter of the network is the minimum number of hops it takes to get from the two furthest nodes on the network. Mathematically this is expressed as:

$$\text{Diameter} = \text{maximum } D_{ij}$$

D_{ij} = shortest path (in links) between the ith and jth node

The same simulation is run again, except this time instead of monitoring the diameter of the network, the *S-I* index is examined. The *S-I* index of a graph is based on the frequency distribution of the shortest path lengths s_{ij} in the graph. It is defined as the pair (S,I), where:

$$S = \frac{\mu_3}{\mu_2} \text{ and } I = \frac{\mu_2}{\mu_1} \tag{5.12}$$

According to Cliff et al. (1979 p. 45) 'The values of the *S* and *I* can be calculated for a variety of theoretical distributions based on the hypergeometric series, and can be mapped on the *S-I* plane.' The resulting *S-I* plane forms a hoop with one end indicating a fully meshed interconnected network and the other a minimally spanning tree. By examining the *S-I* index of the US IP network infrastructure as nodes are removed, one can obtain a quantitative indication of how disconnected the network becomes.

RESULTS

The results of both the diameter and *S-I* index analysis on nodal hierarchies can be found in Tables 5.1 to 5.6.

Table 5.1   Output of diameter and S-I index analysis on binary hierarchies

Diameter	CMSA[1]	$I=u2/u1$	$S=u3/u2$
7		0.2937	0.0499
8	Atlanta	0.3416	0.0927
8	Chicago 1	0.3445	0.0449
8	San Francisco 1	0.3466	0.0424
10	Dallas 2	0.4415	0.4056
10	Washington 1	0.4441	0.3019
10	New York 1	0.4463	0.3133
10	Denver 2	0.4602	0.3656
10	Houston	0.5313	0.4742
10	Kansas City	0.541	0.3871
10	Los Angeles	0.5085	0.2671

10	Cleveland	0.5037	0.2268
10	St. Louis 2	0.5096	0.1999
10	Salt Lake City	0.5069	0.1805
10	Boston 2	0.5145	0.1185
10	Phoenix	0.5374	0.1309

Note [1] Consolidated Metropolitan Statistical Area

Table 5.2   Output of diameter and S-I index analysis on band width hierarchies

Diameter	CMSA[1]	I=u2/u1	S=u3/u2
7		0.2937	0.0499
8	New York 1	0.3029	0.0454
8	Chicago 1	0.3063	-0.0125
8	San Francisco 1	0.3084	-0.0135
9	Dallas 2	0.4029	0.4381
9	Washington 1	0.4086	0.3767
10	Atlanta	0.4442	0.2252
10	Los Angeles	0.4205	0.1234
10	Seattle	0.4188	0.111
10	Denver 2	0.4255	0.1322
10	Kansas City	0.4391	0.086
10	Salt Lake City	0.4376	0.0664
10	Houston	0.4976	0.1549
10	Boston 2	0.553	0.1408
10	Philadelphia	0.5533	0.1429
10	St. Louis 2	0.5624	0.1237

Note [1] As for Table 5.1

Table 5.3   Output of diameter and S-I index analysis on small world regional hierarchies

Diameter	CMSA[1]	I=u2/u1	S=u3/u2
7		0.2937	0.0499
8	New York 1	0.3029	0.0454
8	Chicago 1	0.3063	-0.0125
8	San Francisco 1	0.3155	-0.0468
8	Washington 1	0.3318	-0.0793
9	Boston 2	0.3938	0.2081
10	Dallas 2	0.4804	0.4802
10	Denver 2	0.4962	0.5025
10	St. Louis 2	0.4982	0.489
11	Cleveland	0.5915	0.6812
11	Louisville	0.5933	0.6759
11	Kansas City	0.66	0.5959
12	Seattle	0.7778	0.9118
12	Phoenix	0.7752	0.8822
12	Los Angeles	0.7622	0.881
12	Atlanta	0.7656	0.4362

Note [1] As for Table 5.1

Table 5.4   Output of diameter and S-I index analysis on small world distance hierarchies

Diameter	CMSA[1]	I=u2/u1	S=u3/u2
7		0.2937	0.0499
8	Salt Lake City	0.2935	0.0399
8	Denver 2	0.3003	0.0573
8	San Francisco 1	0.3061	0.0246
9	Dallas 2	0.4081	0.5258
9	Seattle	0.4072	0.5149
9	Chicago 1	0.4194	0.4465
9	Los Angeles	0.3841	0.28
10	Atlanta	0.4205	0.1839

10	Washington 1	0.442	0.0249
10	New York 1	0.4394	-0.1134
10	Phoenix	0.4583	-0.0784
11	Houston	0.541	0.152
13	Miami	0.7341	0.6719
14	Boston 2	0.9572	0.8135
16	Kansas City	1.321	1.1954

Note [1] As for Table 5.1

Table 5.5   Output of diameter and S-I index analysis on global hierarchies

Diameter	CMSA[1]	I=u2/u1	S=u3/u2
7		0.2937	0.0499
8	San Francisco 1	0.2981	0.0258
8	Atlanta	0.3489	0.0779
8	Chicago 1	0.3518	0.0169
10	Dallas 2	0.4384	0.3208
10	Denver 2	0.4503	0.3691
10	Washington 1	0.4717	0.1825
10	New York 1	0.4672	0.057
10	Salt Lake City	0.4649	0.0189
10	Los Angeles	0.442	-0.0806
10	Houston	0.4932	-0.0264
11	Kansas City	0.5306	-0.019
11	Seattle	0.5317	-0.0705
12	Phoenix	0.6464	0.2665
13	Boston 2	0.8097	0.3425
16	Miami	1.3219	1.1954

Note [1] As for Table 5.1

Table 5.6　Output of diameter and S-I index analysis on relay node hierarchies

Diameter	MSA[2]	I=u2/u1	S=u3/u2
7		0.2937	0.0499
8	Kansas City	0.2958	0.0405
8	Salt Lake City	0.2956	0.0302
8	Indianapolis	0.2949	0.0227
8	Seattle	0.2942	0.0137
10	Portland	0.3654	0.6527
10	Sacramento	0.3834	0.7821
10	St. Louis	0.3866	0.7927
10	Denver	0.4063	0.747
10	Atlanta	0.4248	0.5493
10	Washington-Baltimore	0.4254	0.4537
10	Chicago	0.4285	0.302
10	Philadelphia	0.4291	0.297
10	Orlando	0.4412	0.2912
12	Jacksonville	0.5249	0.6122
12	Phoenix	0.5237	0.6021

Note [1] Metropolitan Statistical Area

EXPERIMENT 1 RESULTS

The diameter results are the easiest to interpret, and reveal some interesting findings. The hierarchies with the largest effect on the diameter of the network were the small world distance hierarchy and the global hierarchy, both of which ended in a diameter of 16 when the top 15 nodes (roughly 10 percent) were removed. The superior performance of the small world distance algorithm confirmed that the best performing algorithm would be one based on Euclidean distance. The global hierarchy was based on the presence of a large number of long distance links between two different regions. While it did not directly use Euclidean distance there is an obvious correlation between global links among different regions and a longer physical length.

The starting diameter of the network in the case of both the small world distance and global hierarchy algorithms was 7, and the end result of 16 was more than a doubling of the diameter, meaning it took more than twice the number of hops to reach the two furthest places on the network. This results in a ripple effect across the network where it will take a minimum of twice the time to get from any point to another. This does not take into account the capacity of the links removed and how traffic will be redistributed across the network. This is an area of ongoing research based on this study. While both hierarchies end up at 16, the global hierarchy accelerates more rapidly in the beginning while the small world distance hierarchy increases the diameter more quickly at the end of the nodal hierarchy. The next group of nodal hierarchies was the relay node and small world regional hierarchy, which both end with a diameter of 12. Finally, the binary and bandwidth capacity hierarchy had the least impact, each ending in a diameter of 10.

The diameter relationship of the hierarchies is seen more clearly when all the nodal hierarchies are plotted with their diameters at each successive node removal.

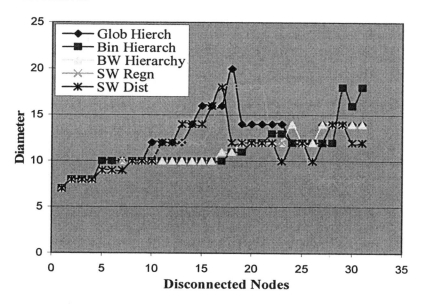

Figure 5.3   Comparison of the diameter effects of nodal hierarchies

The lower impact of the binary and bandwidth hierarchy is clearly evident up to roughly the fifteenth node removal, when the diameter starts to vary erratically first for small world distance, then global, and finally small world regional. The decrease in diameter results from the network Balkanizing into two or more sub-graphs. The sub-graph is a smaller subset of the whole network and thus has a lower diameter. This is a significant juncture because individual places are no longer just being disconnected, but entire islands of nodes are being created, signifying a catastrophic failure of the network. Further, the bottom placement of the binary connectivity hierarchy is of note, since this is the method by which nodes have been chosen for removal in the majority of studies in the literature (Albert et al. 2000, Callaway et al. 2000, Cohen et al. 2001). This would appear to indicate that the most critical nodes in the network are not the most obvious ones, and judging nodes by only the agglomeration of links is not a sufficient method for examining the susceptibility of spatial networks. The study does reveal that incorporating distance into an analysis of critical nodes for network survivability produces significantly improved results. Finally, when it comes to the survivability of the Internet, distance is hardly dead!

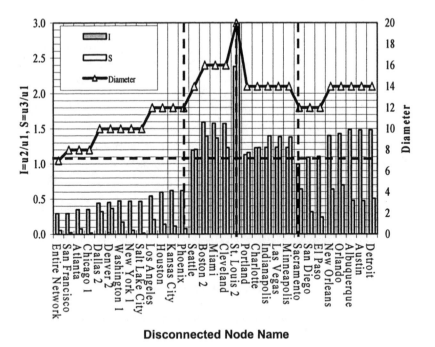

Figure 5.4   Global hierarchy: S and I index and diameter of the network

EXPERIMENT 2 RESULTS

It should also be noted that the point at which the network loses its integrity with the best performing algorithm is considerably higher than previous studies. Previous work (Callaway et al. 2000) notes that the network loses its integrity when the top 4 percent of nodes are removed, but in this simulation network, integrity is not lost until 10.9 percent of nodes are removed. One key difference in approach is that the network was modeled in this exercise with all networks interconnecting with all other networks in the city-to-city matrix. This is not the reality of current network interconnection but the findings point to the increased resiliency that more widespread interconnection brings to the network as a whole. This result confirms that increased interconnection in the network would also increase the resiliency of the network. While interconnection on such a large scale is not economically feasible for the majority of networks because of current peering policies, it should be noted that efforts to build frameworks for inter-network cooperation in times of emergencies would be of great benefit.

An examination of the *S-I* index confirms the findings of the diameter analysis. Figure 5.4 illustrates the *S* and *I* measure of the network as nodes are removed from the network, specifically the global hierarchy approach.

The graph clearly shows the similar effect *S* and *I* have with diameter as nodes are removed and the extreme sensitivity of *S* to network changes. The graphical approach is different from the typical plotting of the *S* and *I* onto the *S-I* plane as (*X,Y*) coordinates, but works well in this case, both to demonstrate the connection between diameter and the *S-I* measures, and to show how increases in the *S-I* index are indicators of a disconnecting network.

PHYSICAL DISJOINT ANALYSIS

The methodology and approaches outlined thus far have only dealt with one facet of US infrastructure, networks that operate with Internet protocol (IP). These IP networks are operational constructs and their topology is logical, not physical. The nodes in an IP network are physical places but the way they are connected is not the actual physical route along which information travels. The map of a typical IP network will show direct connections between far-flung places like New York and San Francisco or Seattle and Chicago. The logical connections of IP networks are carried over physical fiber in the ground, which form much different network constructs. Physical fiber networks typically run over rights of way established by physical transportation networks – roads, railroads, pipelines, or sewers. Fiber is laid, connecting several cities and then leased either to provide connectivity to other networks or to run the networks of the fiber provider. These operational networks then choose from a variety of protocols and technologies to set up an operational network to connect their key assets. The most popular current protocol is IP and the most popular network is the Internet, but there is a wide variety of other protocols and networks that utilize the leased lines of physical fiber networks, such as those utilized by the financial and military communities. A wide variety of critical infrastructures depend on leased lines for their operation, ranging from banking and finance to military command and control. The aggregate private leased lines in the United States dwarf the bandwidth available on the Internet – in 1997 leased lines accounted for 330 Gbps, and the Internet only 75 Gbps (Coffman and Odlyzko 1998). This relationship has only intensified with the telecom boom and bust:

> with very few exceptions all ISPs have typically just a single OC48 or at most OC192 link along their major routes. Yet the facilities based carriers typically have between 40 and 800 fibers along each route, and each fiber is usually capable (with current DWDM technology) of carrying 80 OC48 or OC192 wavelengths. Thus only a small fraction of the fiber capacity is currently used for Internet traffic (Odlyzko 2001, p.13).

The vast majority of this capacity remains unused or is allocated to private leased lines. In fact, the average lit bandwidth used for the Internet is only 1.37 percent of the total for the top 20 US metropolitan areas (based on Telegeography 2002). While the Internet is a small percentage of total capacity it is a much larger percentage of traffic, averaging 2,500-4,000 TB a month compared to 3,000-5,000 TB a month for private lines (Coffman and Odlyzko 1998). As such, the Internet is a good indicator of a very active operational network.

The often-confusing part is that the Internet is a collection of interconnected private lines and networks. The difference between the categories outlined by Coffman and Odlyzko (1998) is that the Internet runs on TCP/IP and the individual private networks (autonomous systems) agree to interconnect with each other under a common framework. However, private lines, as classified, are not openly accessible for interconnection under a common framework and protocol. This still leaves the problem of how one analyzes a network that has two components, one physical and one logical, with two different topologies. One approach is physical disjoint analysis developed by Bhandari (1999), where a logical network is overlaid on the physical network it runs over. In this graph theoretical construct a new terminology is added, spans and span nodes. Spans are the actual physical links that comprise the network, and logical links are built from these spans. Thus, a given span can be common to a number of links, and several spans can combine to form a single logical link (Bhandari 1999). Once a physical and logical network is combined, there are logical links, nodes, and span links. This approach makes more sense when illustrated visually. Figure 5.5 is the physical fiber network for Genuity and Figure 5.6 is the logical IP network that runs over the physical fiber network.

In Figure 5.7 the non-straight lines are spans and the straight lines are the logical links that utilize the spans underneath them. As seen in Figure 5.7 many logical links will often utilize the same span.

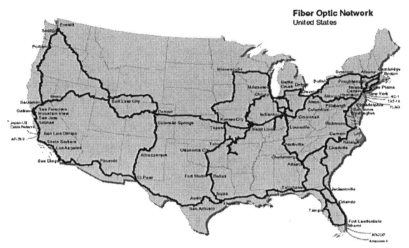

Source: www.genuity.com 2002.

Figure 5.5   Genuity's physical fiber network

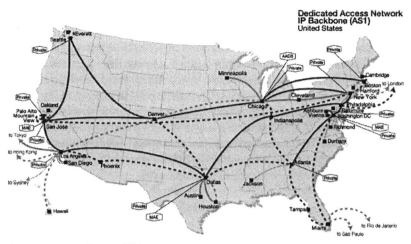

Source: www.genuity.com 2002.

Figure 5.6   Genuity's logical IP network

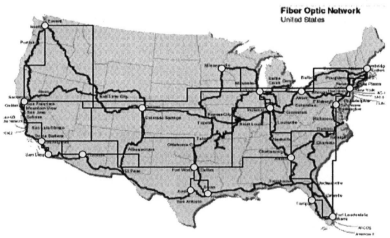

Source: Author's own work.

Figure 5.7   Physical disjoint visualization of Genuity's network

The goal of physical disjoint analysis is to examine these two networks as graphs and to determine how many physically disjoint paths exist between any two places on the network. Thus, if there were a physical fiber cut would there be another physical path for the data to follow to take it to its destination? Mathematically, the edge disjointness (ED) for a pair of paths can be defined as:

$$ED = 1 - \frac{\sum l_j}{\sum l_i} \tag{5.13}$$

where the j sum is over the common edges of the two paths and the i sum is over the edges of the two paths.

This approach becomes clearer when framed as a visual example. In the Genuity example (Figures 5.5 to 5.7), how many physically disjoint paths are there between San Francisco and New York? While there is a direct connection between San Francisco and New York in the logical network, it requires a minimum of 7 physical links to connect the two. There is also a second route that does not use any links in the 7-link path, comprising a completely physically disjoint path with 11 links. Thus its ED would be 1, since there are no common edges shared between the two. If there was a shared path, the ED would be $1 - (1/11+7) = 0.944$. While this approach provides a good tool for examining specific routes, it does not give any insight to the system dynamics of the network or the criticality of links in a route. Building upon the ED approach the two physically disjoint paths illustrated between San Francisco and New York were analyzed to see what the impact of two strategic cuts would have on the logical network. One cut was made between Denver and Kansas on the 7-link disjoint path and the other cut between El Paso and Houston on the 11-link route. Cut one results in the loss of 8 logical connections and cut two results in the loss of two logical connections and the disconnection of the East and West coast. This provides only the characteristic for the routes between two nodes. In order to examine how critical these two links are for the entire network, a link frequency analysis was constructed. This approach analyzes the frequency at which a particular link must be traversed for each iteration of a network until the diameter of the network is reached. Thus, the first iteration would examine how many times link x would have to be traversed in all combinations of two-hop routes, and the third iteration would be the percentage of times a link had to be traversed for all three-hop combinations and so on, until the diameter was reached. When this analysis was run for the two links under examination in the Genuity fiber network, the results were as shown in Table 5.7.

Table 5.7   Link frequency analysis for the Genuity fiber network

	2 hops	3 hops	4 hops	5 hops
Denver – Kansas	5	11	18	23
El Paso	4	8	19	24
Both Cuts	9	19	37	47
Total Paths	60	79	95	97
% of Total	**0.15**	**0.24**	**0.39**	**0.48**

	6 hops	7 hops	8 hops	Total
Denver – Kansas	34	34	23	148
El Paso	27	31	15	128
Both Cuts	61	65	38	276
Total Paths	86	67	38	522
% of Total	**0.71**	**0.97**	**1.00**	**0.53**

The results show that for all two-hop combinations in the network, the two links are utilized in 15 percent of routes. This number increases for each iteration of the network until 97 percent of all routes utilize these two links for all 7-hop combinations, and 100 percent of all 8-hop combinations are dependent on these two links. This approach can also be used to rank the relative importance of links of the network and calculate how many logical connections are dependent on them as illustrated earlier.

VULNERABILITY ANALYSIS OF PHYSICAL FIBER

Often, physical fiber data cannot be converted into nodes and edges. This is especially true for data presented in geographic information systems (GIS) that show the exact physical route that fiber takes along various rights of way (such as highways, rail, gas pipe lines). While the physical location data is very specific, it is impossible to know what parts of the fiber are nodes for interconnection or routing, or even who is leasing the fiber and how it is being utilized. While this physical fiber is the backbone for almost every sector's communications system, including banking, finance, government, military, and emergency response, it cannot be analyzed with the algorithms outlined in the previous methodology section.

In order to analyze physical fiber, a grid approach implemented through a GIS platform is proposed. While it is not possible to identify the operational links and nodes in physical fiber data, there are several other attributes that can be utilized within a particular data set. Specifically the capacity or density of fiber running along any particular conduit can be utilized. If any data set has an attribute for the density or capacity of a physical line passing through a geographic area approach, then a grid density analysis can be performed. A grid density analysis lays a grid over the geographic area of interest. The size of the grid can be scaled to create the granularity of analysis needed for any size geography. Once the grid has been created at a layer in the GIS, then for each individual grid cell the density of fiber is calculated. This can be done in several ways but for this proposed analysis it is the number of individually owned fiber lines in the grid cell. The lines are turned into points and the number of points in each grid cell is calculated. Next the number of geographical diverse paths across the cell is calculated and is used to create a ratio of geographic diversity to fiber density. Areas with high amounts of density but low amounts of diversity will have high numbers, and indicate areas of vulnerability. The data sets utilized for this analysis are 1) a long haul fiber data set for the entire United States obtained from Platts Inc. Telcomap product, and 2) a metropolitan fiber data set for the San Diego central business district obtained from Bandwidth Bay, a joint project of the Downtown San Diego Partnership and Center City Development Corporation. When the grid density approach was applied to the United States data set, the output seen in Figure 5.8 was produced.

EXPERIMENT 3 RESULTS

The output in Figure 5.8 was generated as a three-dimensional image, with the highest peaks and lightest shades indicating the highest densities of fiber with the least amount of geographic diversity. While most of the peaks correlate with large metropolitan areas – most notably Atlanta, San Francisco, Chicago, and Dallas – there are also many areas of high density connecting large cities. This can be seen more clearly when populated areas are layered on top of the fiber density mapping (see Figure 5.9). The dots are color coded, with the highest populated places being gray and the lower populated places being white.

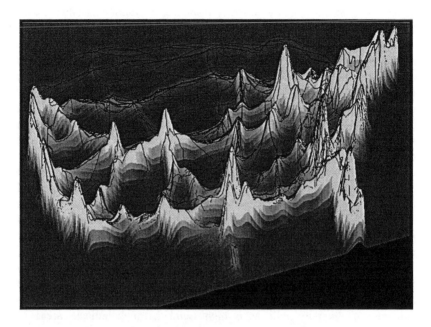

Figure 5.8   3-D US fiber density analysis and visualization

Figure 5.9   Correlation of fiber density with population

Figure 5.10   Fiber density analysis for the San Diego central business district

These areas of high density and low population are especially apparent on East to West routes across the United States. The presence of high fiber densities with low diversity indicates areas of vulnerability that are not located in areas with high population, and also supports the fact that there are dense fiber vulnerabilities in areas of low population. Notable routes include the area connecting Denver and Salt Lake City, Los Angeles-San Francisco, Houston-Los Angeles, and the area north of Orlando. Within metropolitan areas the case is somewhat different; fiber densities are greatest in the central business districts, as illustrated in the Figure 5.10 image of San Diego.

The San Diego image vividly illustrates the strongest fiber densities, depicted by the gray splotches in the heart of the central business district. The two images illustrate the flexibility of the fiber heat-mapping tool to work at a wide range of geographic scales and reveal patterns in the fiber data.   The national map illustrated vulnerabilities in remote areas connecting large metropolitan regions, while the San Diego map illustrates how the agglomeration effect of business location drives fiber density location.   Appendix 1 lists the wired buildings in the San Diego central business district.   The agglomeration of wired businesses accounts for

7,252,300 square feet of rentable office space with an average vacancy rate of only 7.23 percent. The fiber to service these buildings and businesses then must agglomerate along the rights of way traversing the San Diego central business district, producing the distinct fiber densities seen in Figure 5.10.

CONCLUSIONS

Identifying and determining the location of vital nodes in US critical infrastructure has taken on renewed importance since the events of 9/11. The critical infrastructure of today's economy has grown from transport and utilities to include information networks like the Internet, telecommunications, and various financial networks. These networks are structurally different from traditional infrastructure networks, and this chapter has endeavored to develop new methods of identifying critical nodes and links in them. The new approaches developed have a far greater impact on the connectivity of the network than traditional approaches. Interestingly, distance based approaches (the small world distance model and the global hierarchy model) had the greatest impact on the network, and outperformed traditional measures (accessibility and capacity models) by 62.5 percent. That is, these results reveal the important role distance plays in the structural properties of small world and scale-free networks, especially in the case on information infrastructure networks. The result also illustrated that the algorithm based on Euclidean distance performed best among the set of tested algorithms. Further testing should be attempted to discover if better algorithms could be developed or optimized, but this is an encouraging first step. Also of note is the reoccurring importance of 300 miles as a threshold in distance analysis of information networks. It was the critical inflection point between global and local in this study, the average length of leased lines in the Coffman and Odlyzko (1998) study, and the average logical link length in this study. It would appear that, in the case of vulnerability, distance has avenged the premature calls of its demise (Cairncross 1997).

A second finding of interest is that overall the network appears to be more resilient than indicated by previous studies carried out at the router and AS level. The network did not become balkanized into large sub-graphs until 16 nodes (10.9 percent) were removed – a much higher number than the 4 percent indicated by previous studies. One important distinction for this study is that the network was modeled with all networks interconnecting with all other networks in every city. This finding confirmed that a greater level of interconnection in this network increased the resiliency of the network vis-à-vis previously tested networks. This level of interconnection is not the reality of current network practice, but points to the resiliency benefits that broader interconnection brings, and the critical importance of inter-provider routing cooperation in times of emergencies.

This analysis has also put forward a preliminary method of analyzing the interactions of physical and logical networks. Utilizing the concept of spans from Bhandari (1999) it is possible to perform physical disjoint analysis and to determine the impact of physical fiber cuts on a logical network. The approach was extended to allow an overall system analysis to determine the criticality of physical links to the operation of a logical network. This allows vulnerability analysis of operational networks and the private line infrastructure they are dependent on at both a micro and macro level. This is a first step in analyzing the interdependencies of various information networks (financial, military, aviation, energy) and the fiber infrastructure they are dependent on.

Finally a physical fiber vulnerability heat-mapping tool is introduced. The heat-mapping tool provides analysis of physical fiber when nodal methods are not possible. Further, the tool can be calibrated to work at a variety of geographic scales ranging from the national level to the city block. Analysis with the tool illustrates possible vulnerable locations where limited rights of way have caused an agglomeration of fiber with a low level of diversity. These vulnerable areas could be single points of failure that could affect multiple critical infrastructures. Often these vulnerabilities are not in large metropolitan areas, which are usually highlighted as targets, but instead in areas of low or no population, which are very difficult to defend. The finding of significant vulnerabilities along remote East-West fiber routes supports the final hypothesis of this chapter that there are dense fiber vulnerabilities in areas of low population.

POLICY PRESCRIPTIONS

Applying the analysis of this chapter to create public policy recommendations proves to be a difficult task. Unlike traditional infrastructures, fiber networks are almost entirely held by private firms. Multiple providers supply the infrastructure, often interconnecting with each other and always in tight competition, creating unique interdependencies. One network's security is only as good as the other networks it connects with (Kunreuther et al. 2002). Thus there is no direct economic incentive to secure a network if it can be compromised by the competition; a classic case of the prisoner's dilemma (Kunreuther et al.

2002). In a telecommunications industry experiencing its largest economic downturn in history, the incentive for security is only further pushed to the background. This raises the question of whether a policy intervention is needed if the market is not fulfilling the role of providing adequate security. This question goes outside the scope of this chapter, but the analysis does suggest some fundamental recommendations that should be fulfilled by the market or a policy intervention:

1. Technological and market forces have reduced available reserve capacity and the number of geographically diverse routing paths.
2. Failure of single links and nodes can have serious repercussions and having backup providers is not always a safe solution.
3. Operational networks need to be mapped to physical networks to determine susceptibilities.

The best way to secure information networks against cyber and physical attack remains an open question, with large implications for the US economy and national security.

NOTE

1. A Loschian landscape is in reference to the work of Augustus Losch, which posited that the size and distribution of markets and service centers varies according to relative size and location.

6. Packets and Power:
The Interdependency of Infrastructure

The last chapter covered methods and approaches to quantifying the vulnerability of information infrastructure networks, both physical and logical. Information networks, though, do not operate in a vacuum; they are interdependent with other infrastructures for their operation. The most obvious example is the dependency of information infrastructure on electric power. Without electric powers computers cannot operate. The importance of critical infrastructure has become all the more prominent because of the possibility of it being exploited by terrorists for attack:

> The vulnerability of societies to terrorist attacks results in part from the proliferation of chemical, biological, and nuclear weapons of mass destruction, but it is also a consequence of the highly efficient and interconnected systems we rely on for key services such as transportation, information, energy, and health care. The efficient functioning of these systems reflects great technological achievements of the past century, but interconnectedness within and across systems also means that infrastructures are vulnerable to local disruptions, which could lead to widespread or catastrophic failures (NRC 2002, p.1)

In short the National Research Council (NRC) report on making the nation safer illustrates the recurring theme that private efficiencies are resulting in public vulnerabilities (Branscomb forthcoming). Often times these vulnerabilities are not independent but result from the interconnection and interdependency of multiple critical infrastructures. To begin to tackle the issue of interdependency it is useful to examine how infrastructures are different and how they are interdependent at the same time. As a case study for the approach this chapter examines two critical infrastructures, power and information. The third chapter of this book outlined where both information networks and power networks have failed. Whether the failure was the result of intentionally malicious acts, like the attack on the World Trade Center, or accidental failures like the August 2003 Northeast blackout there are significant and demonstrated repercussions and losses. Understanding the interdependency of critical infrastructures and the impacts from failures is a crucial link in understanding the topic and formulating adequate policy to address it. This chapter presents two approaches to investigating multiThe first approach is a topological study of differences between two critical infrastructures, namely the control interconnection network for the electric power grid and the city-to-city IP network used in Chapter 5. Once the differences between the networks are illustrated, a more granular analysis attempts to analyze the geographic interdependencies of the electric power grid and physical fiber infrastructure of the United States through the use of a novel interdependency vulnerability mapping tool.

The fourth chapter of the book outlined mechanics that have been developed to examine complex networks such as the electric power grid and the Internet. One of the key diagnostic tools outlined in that literature was the examination of network connectivity distributions. Albert et al. (2000) point out that scale-free networks, with power law connectivity distributions like the Internet, are resilient to random failures but highly susceptible to targeted attacks. An examination of the literature on the topic leads to the conclusion that the more skewed the connectivity distribution, the higher the level of hubbing, and the higher the level of vulnerability. In a scale-free network there is a small minority of nodes that have the vast majority of connections. As was seen in Figure 4.2, in the scale-free (power law) network, more than 60 percent of nodes can be reached from the five most connected nodes, compared with only 27 percent in the exponential network. As network connectivity distributions move away from a power law to an exponential connectivity distribution, the top most-connected nodes have a smaller minority of the connections in the network. Thus it would seem safe to assume when those most-connected nodes fail in an exponential network it would not have as large an impact as the same failures in a network with a power law connectivity distribution. In short, the theory points to an exponential network being more resilient than a scale-free network.

What makes this theoretical discussion about the resiliency of different connectivity distributions interesting is the fact that the electric power grid network has been reported to have an exponential connectivity distribution, while the Internet is reported to be scale-free with a power law connectivity distribution. Thus, following the train of logic just presented, the power grid should be more resilient than the Internet. To test this assertion an aggregated power grid and Internet set of network data is presented. This is then followed by an examination of the connectivity distributions of each infrastructure network and simulations examining the resiliency of these networks to targeted node failures. This will be followed by a spatial analysis of the networks utilizing a grid density approach for vulnerability mapping. In addition to density maps for each infrastructure, a density map combining power and information networks is presented to examine geographic interdependencies.

METHODOLOGY

In order to first delineate the differences between information and power networks it is useful to examine their connectivity distributions as a first step for analysis. The literature illustrates that the connectivity distributions can provide some insight into structural characteristics of networks. For this analysis, two data sets were used for comparison. For the testing of information networks, a dataset of aggregated IP[1] network providers from the year 2000 is used, comprising a matrix of 147 metropolitan statistical areas and the connectivity between each one (Malecki 2002). As stated in Chapter 5, it should be noted that the accuracy of the IP data is imperfect. IP network providers' maps often advertise more capacity than is currently in operation, and future routes are often shown as current routes. The power data is culled from the control area interconnection network, which delineates the physical transmission and interconnection of power between geographic areas in North America (Platts 2004). The control interconnection network is composed of 147 interconnection nodes and is decomposed into a connectivity matrix for comparison with the IP matrix.

Utilizing these two matrices, accessibility indexes were created for each node in the network:

$$A_i = \sum_{i=1}^{n} d_{ij} \tag{6.1}$$

The accessibility numbers for each node were then rank ordered and plotted as log-log distributions. The connectivity distributions for the power control network and IP network are presented in Figure 6.2.

The control and IP network present two distinct connectivity distributions. The IP network is a power law distribution while the power control network is an exponential distribution, or in the Amaral et al. (2000) classification, a single scale network. The connectivity distributions of these two spatial networks are similar to non-spatial analysis seen in the literature. The Internet at the router and autonomous system level (Faloutsos et al. 1999) has power law connectivity distributions, which are very similar to the connectivity distribution seen in the IP city-to-city network. Also, the US power grid (transmission lines and substations) and US Western power grid (Watts and Strogatz 1998) have been found to be exponential single scale networks, all very similar to the exponential distribution seen above. It should be noted that both power control network and IP network are aggregated networks that represent a higher level of the network and comprise a smaller number of nodes, yet they still retain the same structural characteristics as at a more granular level.

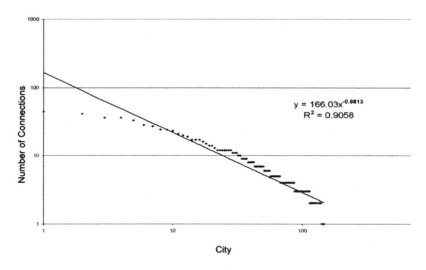

Figure 6.1   Connectivity distribution for the IP backbone network

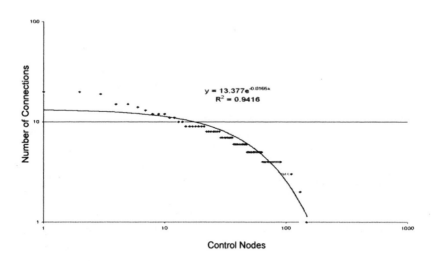

Figure 6.2   Connectivity distribution for the electric power grid control area network

In order to test the resiliency and vulnerability of each of these networks, a failure simulation is run. A node failure scenario is run for both networks, where each node is successively removed according to its accessibility rank. In both scenarios after each node is failed, the diameter of the network is measured.

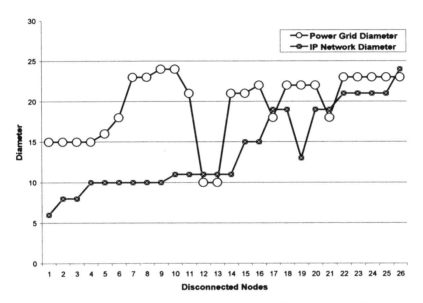

Figure 6.3   Comparative network failures for the power grid and IP backbone network

Figure 6.3 illustrates the diameter of both the power grid and IP city-to-city network as the top most-connected nodes are failed. The starting points of both networks are as would be expected. The diameter of the IP network is considerably less than the diameter of the power grid network. The connectivity distribution of the IP network indicates a higher level of connectivity to the top most-connected hubs, which accounts for its lower diameter and high efficiency. This efficiency theoretically comes with a price: vulnerability to targeted attacks on the most highly connected nodes. Previous studies have stated that scale-free networks with power law distributions are 'more sensitive' to targeted node removal than ER or WS models with exponential distributions (Holme et al. 2002). The results of this test, though, illustrate a much different finding. The IP city-to-city network with a power law connectivity distribution was more resilient than the power grid network with an exponential connectivity distribution. This result contradicts what would be assumed and stated by the literature. Why has such a discrepancy resulted?

The most feasible answer is that connectivity distributions do not tell the whole story about the topology of a network. In fact, there is a very wide variety of different topologies that could result in a power law or exponential connectivity distribution. Further, it would appear from these results that some of these distributions are more resilient than others. In this case the topology of the IP city-to-city was one of the more resilient topologies possible with a power law connectivity distribution, while the power grid network was one of the more vulnerable topologies possible from an exponential connectivity distribution. This possibility of a range of topologies poses an interesting opportunity. It is possible that an efficient network could also be optimized to be more resilient. Somewhere in the spectrum of topologies possible within a power law connectivity distribution is one that maximizes efficiency and resiliency. This is an avenue of research that has generated momentum under the idea of highly optimized tolerance (HOT), specifically in regard to more accurate models of the Internet (Alderson et al. 2003). If the characteristics of topologies that allow an increase in resiliency while maintaining efficiency could be identified mathematically, it would be a significant and helpful finding. If this can be accomplished, it could be possible to link economic and policy incentives to mechanisms that would increase the resiliency of networks without a loss of efficiency. This is one possible approach to resolving the overarching problem of private efficiencies creating public vulnerabilities.

VULNERABILITY ANALYSIS OF PHYSICAL FIBER AND TRANSMISSION LINES

As was illustrated in the previous chapter, there are many circumstances where network data cannot be converted into nodes and edges. This is especially true for data presented in geographic information systems (GIS) that show the exact physical route that network lines take. Also when you have extremely large networks such as the US power grid, with 14,099 substations and 19,657 transmission lines, it becomes computationally difficult to look at anything other than binary connectivity, precluding issues such as density and capacity. Lastly, it is not obvious that there is a matrix approach to analyzing the interdependency of power networks and information networks, largely because of a lack of interconnection and dependency data.

In order to analyze physical fiber and power transmission lines, a grid approach implemented through a GIS platform is proposed that builds on the demonstration in the previous chapter. To quickly reprise the approach, it is not always possible to identify nodes and links in physical network data, but there are several other attributes that can be utilized within a particular data set for analysis. Specifically the capacity or density of network links can be utilized. If any data set has an attribute for the density or capacity of a physical line passing through a geographic area then a grid density analysis can be performed. The data sets utilized for this analysis are a long haul fiber data set for the entire United States and Canada obtained from Platts Inc. Telcomap product and the transmission line data set for US and Canada obtained from Platts Inc. Powermap.

Using the grid density analysis on the fiber optic grid data produced the results seen in Figure 6.4.

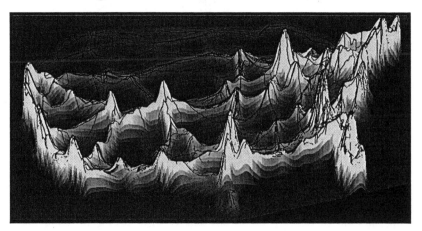

Figure 6.4   A fiber density analysis of North America

The fiber optic grid analysis illustrates an interesting density topology discussed in the previous chapter. For the sake of comparison with the electric power grid analysis, some additional features will be highlighted. There are several tall spikes in large urban areas such as Chicago, San Francisco, Dallas, Atlanta, and the Boston-Washington corridor. All these areas fit the previous literature as large consumers of information services and locations of agglomeration of communications infrastructure. There are also areas of high density and low diversity connecting urban areas. This is especially true in the western half of the US where two routes accommodate the majority of fiber density.

The same approach can now be applied to the US electric power grid for comparison, as seen in Figure 6.5

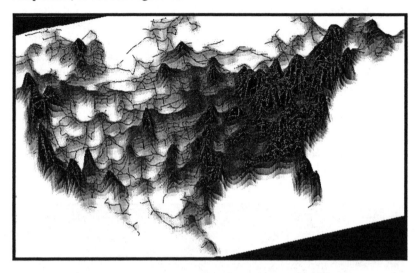

Figure 6.5   A power transmission line density analysis of North America

The density topology of the electric power grid is distinctly different from the fiber optic grid. The distribution of power lines is far more uniform than that found in the fiber optic grid. This makes intuitive sense, since the demand for power is far more uniform than the demand for high-end information services that require high-speed fiber optic connectivity. The more distributed spatial nature of the power grid also prevents the high concentration of density across any one or two links connecting urban agglomerations. One aspect of note in the power grid analysis is the high density of transmission lines found in the middle of Ohio. The exceedingly high density of transmission lines in Ohio is more distinctly illustrated in Figure 6.6

The high density of transmission lines in Ohio is of particular interest because this is close to the location where the August 2003 blackout originated. The correlation between the density of transmission lines and blackouts is an area that warrants further investigation.

With density analysis of both the fiber optic grid and electric power grid presented, it is now useful to see what kind of spatial interdependencies occur between the two. In order to accomplish this task, both data sets were combined in the GIS platform and the grid density analysis was run on both overlapping layers. The outcome is presented in Figure 6.7.

Figure 6.6   Transmission line density analysis illustrating the prominence of Ohio

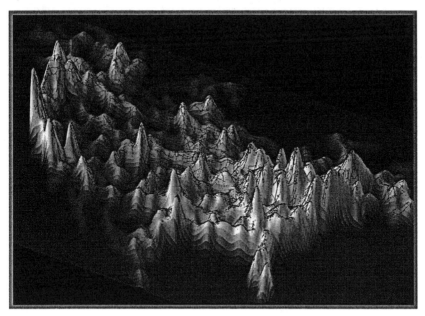

Figure 6.7   Transmission line and fiber spatial interdependency density analysis

The resulting map illustrates areas where there are high densities of both fiber optic lines and transmission lines. In such areas, a natural disaster or malicious attack would seriously affect both infrastructures. The spatial interdependency map does not have the distinct variation of the fiber map, but there are still distinct areas of density. Chicago, Atlanta, Dallas, and San Francisco are all illustrated as areas of high density for both infrastructures. There are also routes between large urban areas that show high densities, particularly in the Rocky Mountains and the Atlantic coast.

DIRECTIONS FOR FUTURE RESEARCH

The analysis presented in the last two chapters regarding what can be accomplished with GIS-based approaches is just the beginning of what is possible. The grid density approach that has been outlined can be combined with spatial statistics for a variety of analyses. One of the most intriguing is the ability to perform failure simulations on physical infrastructure data such as the telecommunications fiber and power grid data presented earlier. One of the ongoing problems in complex network analysis is the computational difficulty of working with very large weighted networks. A weighted network would include such additional variables as the bandwidth capacity of a fiber link or the voltage capacity of an electric transmission line. When these types of variables are incorporated in the mathematical analyses described in Chapter 4, the size of the network that is computationally manageable is severely bounded.

The grid density approach, though, creates the possibility of overcoming these computational barriers. When a grid is laid over the network data, a cell either has network links going through it or not; as such, the grid can be coded as a contiguity matrix. Further, each cell can be coded beyond just a binary designation to include the weight of the cell based on the number of network links or the sum capacity of the links to the cell. The grid can be sized in accordance with the granularity and sensitivity desired for the analysis. Once the contiguity matrix, weighted or binary, has been produced, a variety of failures can then be produced. If a fiber cut was to be simulated, then a single cell could be removed, or if a powerful bomb blast was the goal, several cells could be removed in accordance with the impact radius of the blast. Once the failure has been accounted for in damaged cells, spatial statistics can be used to calculate the possible impact on the network.

Local effects to the network could be measured with the use of the Local Moran's *I*, Ord-Getis and G*. The Local Moran's *I* statistic, the more commonly used of the two, is defined as follows:

$$I_i = z_i \sum_j w_{ij} z_j \qquad (6.2)$$

where z_i is the weight assigned to cell *I* which could be defined as the density of a particular type of infrastructure, z_j to cell *j* and w_{ij} is the contiguity matrix.

This statistic, in a sense, provides a measure of similarity or dissimilarity of neighboring cells, given assumptions about contiguity and using some measure of intensity.

MEASURING GEOGRAPHIC INTERDEPENDENCIES

With some modification to the Local Moran's *I* statistic, it is possible to identify locations where there are strong interdependencies between the power grid and fiber optic cable. The equation for this is as follows:

$$I_{kl}^i = z_k^i \sum_j W_{ij} z_l^j \qquad (6.3)$$

where z_k^i and z_l^j are the two weights of interest (Anselin 1995).

Interdependencies can also be explored by using a dual kernel density interpolation technique that applies in a single to two distributions rather than one, incorporating the two in a single framework. One of the requirements for using the technique is that a density output be specified. There are four different types of output that can be utilized, although it appears as if what is called the log ratio output measure would be most appropriate when examining the power grid and the fiber optic cable. It is used when one or both of the distributions are spatially skewed. The form of this equation is:

$$LogRatio = Ln\lfloor g(x_j)/ g(y_j)\rfloor \qquad (6.4)$$

where $g(x_j)$ is the density estimate for the first distribution and $g(y_j)$ is the estimate for the second.

EXPLORING ERROR AND ATTACK TOLERANCE

The error and attack tolerance of the power grid and telecommunications infrastructure can also be explored through the use of the Global Moran's I. The Global Moran's I measures the degree of clustering across the entire network, and can be used as a proxy for global connectivity. It takes the following form:

$$I = \frac{n \sum\limits_{i}^{n} \sum\limits_{j}^{n} w_{ij} \left(x_i - \bar{x} \right) \left(x_j - \bar{x} \right)}{\left(\sum\limits_{i}^{n} \sum\limits_{j}^{n} w_{ij} \right) \sum\limits_{i}^{n} \left(x_i - \bar{x} \right)^2} \tag{6.5}$$

where $\bar{x}$ is the mean value of density for the entire set of cells in the study area.

The Global Moran's I could be used to recalculate the global connectivity of the network after a network failure has been simulated. Once a failure simulation has been established, a variety of criticality ranking measures can be used to establish which cells in the grid are most critical. Then an analysis similar to that attempted in Chapter 5 could be undertaken.

CONCLUSIONS

This chapter set out to explore some unresolved problems in the study of critical infrastructure, specifically how critical networks are different and how they are also interdependent. The analysis of how the power grid and IP network structures differed revealed what the literature suggested; the IP network had a power law connectivity distribution and the power grid had an exponential connectivity distribution. The results of running connectivity based nodal failures on both networks, though, resulted in findings contradictory to the literature. The exponential power grid network failed far more quickly than the power law IP network, even though the IP network was more efficient and had a greater level of hubbing. The result indicates that there is a wide variety of possible topologies from any given connectivity distribution. While a connectivity distribution is a useful network measure, it is limited in what it can indicate about the specifics of any one network's topology. The finding is encouraging since it indicates that it is possible to design topologies that are both efficient and more resilient to targeted attacks. Many questions remain to be answered regarding how to optimize networks to bring out both characteristics, and what mechanisms would encourage them.

The second section of this chapter went beyond looking at the difference between networks and examined interdependencies between critical infrastructures, specifically electric power and physical fiber. The grid density tool introduced in Chapter 5 was extended to analyze the spatial interdependency of multiple critical networks. The analysis illustrated areas where there are agglomerations of both electric transmission lines and fiber optic lines that are both constrained by a lack of diversity. Perhaps the most interesting finding came from the analysis of the electric power grid to set up the interdependency analysis. The grid density analysis of the US electric power grid demonstrated that the area with the highest density of transmission lines was also the location of the fault that resulted in the huge 12 August, 2003 blackout. While blackouts and other network failures are often accidental and random in their causes, the geographic location of the failure can have a significant impact on the magnitude of the failure. This is an area in need of further investigation beyond one anecdotal case.

NOTE

1. IP stands for Internet protocol. These networks are the transit backbone networks for Internet traffic.

7. Allocating Scarce Resources for Network Protection

Once it has been determined that a network is vulnerable, it is next important to determine how best to remedy, or guard against those vulnerabilities and protect the network as a whole. The literature of complex networks outlines a few strategies regarding methods of protecting networks, especially those of the scale-free variety. The literature does not, though, examine the cost effectiveness of strategies or real world restraints in implementation. Tight budgets in IT sectors across the globe limit the amount of money that is available for security investment. In a time of diminishing resources to invest in security, what are cost effective strategies of investment? This chapter attempts to fill this gap in the literature by proposing a cost effectiveness approach and how it can be applied to real world policy scenarios. First the protection strategies described in the complex network literature are tested, followed by the introduction of a cost effectiveness tool and the testing of a variety of protection strategies.

Once generic strategies have been tested, real world policy variables are introduced. The first variable introduced is the geography of jurisdiction. Can a policy that only has domestic jurisdiction provide effective protection for the United States? What role does international cooperation play in the protection of interconnected information infrastructure? Finally, two possible cybersecurity strategies are introduced, one for the US federal government and one for the US financial services industry to determine which is the more cost effective policy approach.

METHODOLOGY

In order to accomplish these tasks, the problem is simplified and examined at a macro level. The approach is to examine the AS level topology of the Internet to determine what minimal level of protection will be required to protect the overall health of the network and to prevent the wide-scale spread of generic malicious infections. Most malicious infections spread by email or random IP address probing, and most infection simulations also run at this level of analysis. The problem with this approach at a macro policy and economic level is that there are no economic entities that can be dealt with or that are represented. The email end-user or IP address holders are difficult to identify and even more difficult to coordinate for a protection effort. While the AS level is not technically accurate, it does provide a set of economic actors that can be identified, and it does therefore allow for testing of the policy and economic implications of different protection strategies. The focus here is not on recreating realistic malicious attack scenarios, but on testing realistic protection strategies. Unfortunately data or techniques to fuse the two together have not yet been identified, but realistic worm simulations appear to have been accomplished (Moore et al. 2003; Kephart and White 1991; Zou et al. 2002), but appropriate policy analysis has not.

For this analysis, AS level nodes are selected for protection (that is, when a malicious infection encounters the node, it does not become infected or pass the infection on to others), and the protection strategy is tested to see how it affects the spread of an infection in the network. This approach looks at proactive measures, specifically where to invest limited resources, to stop malicious infections, instead of previous research that examines containing or eliminating existing worms (Pastor-Satorras and Vespignani 2002; Moore et al. 2003). Considering the rapid spread of the SQL Slammer worm this could be a worthwhile path of investigation. The first ASs selected for protection are random, and then selection is based on their connectivity in the network. The threshold of ASs needed for protection is tested to determine at what point an acceptable level of protection has been achieved. If the 'protect the hubs' strategy proves prudent, further tests will be conducted to determine what percentage of hubs is required for a 'least effort strategy' to provide an adequate level of cybersecurity. Since it was not possible to acquire cost data for protection, 'least effort' is simply defined as the minimal number of ASs that need to be protected. It is assumed there would be a wide variation in cost depending on the size of the AS. Further, no attempt is made to determine how these ASs would be protected, and the non-realistic assumption of 100 percent protection is assumed.

DATA

Each node in the network analyzed is an individual autonomous system connected to the Internet. The data for this analysis was obtained from the University of Michigan's Internet Topology Project[1] and is based on data extracted from Oregon Route views on 30 September, 2001 and consists of 11,955 individual autonomous systems. The AS data was then analyzed utilizing two different approaches: a weak and a strong worm. A worm, in this case, is just a generic term for a malicious infection that affects the Internet at a network level, as opposed to a virus, which typically is transmitted through email. The simulation is intended to look at how infections spread from one firm's network to another, and not at the IP address level that worms have used to propagate in the past. The weak worm and strong worm will both be run with a 'protect the hubs' strategy with the most-connected node being protected first, the next most-connected being protected second, and so on. For purposes of simplicity, the protected nodes in these simulations will be referred to as the 'core'. The algorithm for the weak and strong worms is given below.

Weak Worm Algorithm

1. Input: AS network of n nodes.
2. Represent n nodes as a vector $V = [v_1, v_2, ... v_n]$.
3. Assign a value +1 to each node of V so as to identify these nodes as NOT INFECTED.
4. Initialize empty vectors PROTCORE PC, the FIFO queue POTINFECTED PI and reinfection counter r and revisit-protected-core counter u to zero.
5. Initialize immediate neighbor vectors B and S.
6. Pick a random node v_i from V such that $v_i \notin PC$.
7. Remove v_i from V and add it to PROTCORE PC and assign a value of 0 to identify this node as being part of the protected core.
8. Pick a random node v_j from V.
9. Remove node v_j from V and put node v_j in the vector INFECTED I.
10. Assign a value of -1 to v_j.
11. Find immediate neighbors S of v_j and put them in a FIFO queue POTINFECTED PI.
12. While $PI(1) \neq v_j$.
13. Remove first node $k = PI(1)$ from PI.
14. If $k \in PC$, then $u = u + 1$ % Its already in the protected core.
15. Else if $k \in I$ then $r = r + 1$ % Its reinfection.
16. Else add it to vector INFECTED I and assign a value of -1.
17. Find immediate neighbors B of k and add them to FIFO PI.
18. If $PI \neq [\ ]$ (not empty) go to step 12.
19. Else Output: r, u, I and PC and break out of the loop beginning in step 6, else Go to step 6.

Thus, as soon as the infection points back to the very first node that started the infection, the process of infection is stopped.

Strong Worm Algorithm

1.   Input: AS network of n nodes.
2.   Compute the connectivity vector V for a given AS network.
3.   Sort the vector V such that $V = [v_1, v_2, ...v_n]$, where $v_1 > v_2 > ... > v_n$.
4.   Assign a value +1 to each node of V so as to identify these nodes as NOT INFECTED.
5.   Initialize empty vectors PROTCORE PC, the FIFO queue POTINFECTED PI and reinfection counter r and revisit-protected-core counter u to zero.
6.   Initialize immediate neighbor vector B and S.
7.   Select an arbitrary number of top m nodes from V and call this CORE C such that $C = [c_1, c_2, ...c_m]$ where $m << n$.
8.   For $i = 1$ to m pick node c_i from C and put it in PROTCORE PC and assign a value of 0 to identify as being part of the protected core.
9.   Pick a random node v_j from V such that $v_j \notin PC$.
10. Remove node v_j from V and put node v_j in the vector INFECTED.
11. Assign a value of -1 to v_j.
12. Find immediate neighbors S of v_j and put them in a FIFO queue POTINFECTED PI.
13. Remove node $k = PI(1)$ from PI.
14. If $k \in PC$, then $u = u+1$ %% Its already in the protected core.
15. Else if $k \in I$ then $r = r+1$ %% Its reinfection.
16. Else add it to vector INFECTED I and assign a value of -1.
17. Find immediate neighbors B of k and add them to FIFO PI.
18. If $PI \neq [\ ]$ (not empty) go to step 13. Else Output: r, u, I and PC.
19. Go to step 4.

To provide a comparison for the 'protect the hubs' strategy, the strong worm algorithm is run but the protected nodes in the core are chosen randomly, instead of by connectivity. The random strong worm algorithm is as follows.

Strong Worm Random Algorithm

1.   Input: AS network of n nodes.
2.   Represent n nodes as a vector $V = [v_1, v_2, ...v_n]$.
3.   Assign a value +1 to each node of V so as to identify these nodes as NOT INFECTED.
4.   Initialize empty vectors PROTCORE PC, the FIFO queue POTINFECTED PI and reinfection counter r and revisit-protected-core counter u to zero.

5. Initialize immediate neighbor vectors B and S.
6. For a fixed number of iterations.
7. Pick a random node v_i from V such that $v_i \notin PC$.
8. Remove v_i from V and add it to PROTCORE PC and assign a value of 0 to identify as being part of the protected core.
9. Pick a random node v_j from V.
10. Remove node v_j from V and put node v_j in the vector INFECTED I.
11. Assign a value of -1 to v_j.
12. Find immediate neighbors S of v_j and put them in a FIFO queue POTINFECTED PI.
13. Remove first node $k = PI(1)$ from PI.
14. If $k \in PC$, then $u = u + 1$ % Its already in the protected core.
15. Else if $k \in I$ then $r = r + 1$ % Its reinfection.
16. Else add it to vector INFECTED I and assign a value of -1.
17. Find immediate neighbors B of k and add them to FIFO PI.
18. If $PI \neq [\ ]$ (not empty) go to step 12.
19. Else Output: r, u, I and PC.
20. Go to step 5.

RESULTS OF TARGETED VS. RANDOM PROTECTION STRATEGIES

When the weak worm is run, a node is randomly chosen and all of its neighbors are infected. Next, one of those infected neighbors is randomly chosen and all of its neighbors are infected, and the process is repeated until the infection refers back to the originating node. The worm takes a random walk across the network, infecting all the neighbors of each node in its walk. The strong worm, on the other hand, infects all of the neighbors instead of just selecting one node to follow. This allows the worm to infect all ASs in a rapid manner when no protection is in place. To manage the strong worm computationally, a queue approach was used where the neighbors of the originally infected node are put into a queue and infected in turn. As the worm spreads, each neighbor's neighbors are put into the queue and infected as well. This way, the length of the queue, and nodes to be infected, can be plotted along with the total number of infected nodes, total number of attempts to infect nodes per cycle, and the number of times the protected core is visited per cycle. A cycle is simply a single simulation run with n number of nodes protected. The output produced by the simulation takes the worst-case infection scenarios from 15 iterations of each cycle. The results from the weak worm, strong worm, and random weak and strong worm are presented below as Figures 7.1 to 7.4.

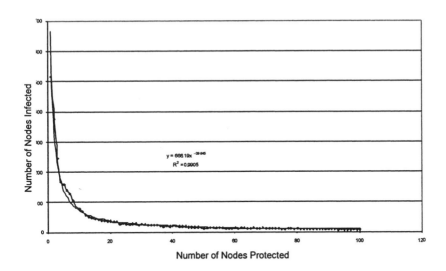

Figure 7.1   The number of nodes protected versus size of worst-case infected cluster

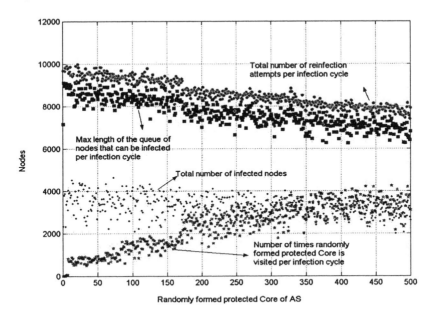

Figure 7.2   The number of nodes protected versus size of infected cluster with random protection strategy and weak worm

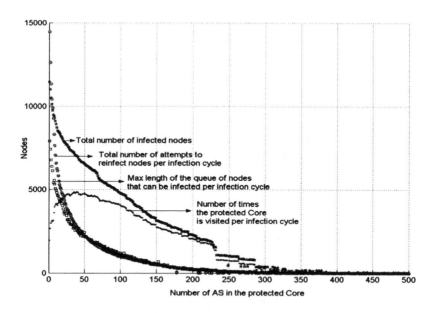

Figure 7.3   The number of nodes protected versus worst-case size of infected cluster over 15 iterations

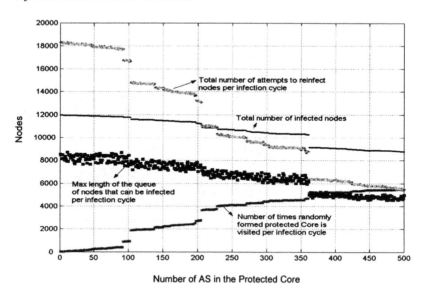

Figure 7.4   The number of nodes protected versus worst-case size of infected cluster with random protection strategy

This approach enables the testing of how increasing the size of the protected core affects the spread of a virus or worm across the network of ASs.   The results of the weak worm in Figure 7.1 illustrate a precipitous drop in infection clusters with the first few nodes protected, and after about 20 nodes are protected, the change in the infection cluster is relatively small.   The sharp shift is indicative of the tight power law fit ($R^2 = 0.9905$) when the data is placed in a log-log format.   The result indicates a distinct point of inflection where there are diminishing returns for further investment in nodal protection.   When this is compared to a random protection strategy with the weak worm, the results are dramatic.   The weak worm infections under the random strategy illustrate a random distribution with little noticeable decrease even after 500 nodes are protected.

EXPERIMENT 1 RESULTS

The result of the strong worm (Figure 7.3) does not show the sharp power law decline seen in the weak worm, but there is still a definitive point where the infection drops off drastically (node 229) and then becomes largely ineffective (node 275).   While the number of nodes requiring protection to contain the worm is larger than the weak worm, the total nodes protected are only 2.3 percent of the total network.

In comparison, when a random protection strategy is implemented (Figure 7.4), little to no protection is afforded even after 500 nodes are protected.   Under the random protection strategy, protecting even 500 nodes results in 8,789 infected nodes, 72.3 percent of the total network.   The one large drop in the results is because AS 701 (Worldcom), the most-connected node in the network, was randomly chosen.   This result supports the belief that a 'defend the hubs' strategy results in fewer infected nodes than a 'random protection' strategy.

The results of this study and the particular simulation approach taken illustrate a significant improvement in security from a 'random protection' strategy, although the 'protect the hubs' strategy becomes less effective as a worm is made more potent.   Ideally, this work needs to be extended to investigate scenarios where protection is not 100 percent and some worms find their way through an AS's defense.   This would provide an additional level of testing for the effectiveness of the strategy.

A COST EFFECTIVENESS ANALYSIS OF CYBERSECURITY STRATEGIES

One of the problems with the analysis implemented so far is that it considers the cost of protecting all autonomous systems to be equal. The cost of protecting a large global network like UUnet with 2,451 connections and a local University with one connection are treated the same. To remedy this problem, a simple cost function is introduced, where the cost of protecting a link connecting two autonomous systems is $1. Unfortunately, better cost figures for malicious attacks on the internet are not available. Several industry experts were consulted, but approaches and cost figures varied widely. Chen (2003) calculated cost and benefits for protection from denial of service attacks, based on the frequency of attacks, number of subscribers, and AT&T's network charge to customers for security services. While the metrics are not appropriate for the analysis here, they did, interestingly, conclude that providing DOS protection services would be profitable strategy for ISPs (Chen 2003).

Under the $1 per link cost structure the total cost of protecting a network will then be the total number of links multiplied by $1. From the prior analysis of security strategies the most successful will be taken and the total cost of that strategy calculated. Suppose that the total budget for securing nodes/links is B \$, and assume that it takes a fixed cost of C \$ to secure each link connected to a set of nodes, then the total number of nodes/links that can be secured with a budget of B \$ is given by the following relation:

$$\sum_{i=1}^{n} L_i \times C \leq B \qquad (7.1)$$

where L_i is the number of links associated with node i, and n is the total number of nodes. Once the cost of the strategy has been determined, the return on investment of that strategy will be compared to other strategies. Once a set of protected nodes has been defined for each strategy, the strong worm algorithm will be run for each. Once the algorithm has been run, the following data will be collected:

- Number of infected nodes
- Number of non-infected links
- Cost effectiveness ratio
- Number of protected nodes
- Number of protected links

- The protected link multiplier = number of protected nodes / number of protected links
- The integrity of the network after node failures are accounted for.

This data enables an examination of the return on investment for different allocations of resources to protect the network. The money invested will be the same, but the outcome will differ by the investment strategy. When the cost for the 'protect the hubs' strategy was calculated with the top 276 nodes protected, using the equation outlined above, the total cost of protection was $19,544. The testing of the 'protect the hubs' strategy illustrated it as having maximum benefit with the least number of nodes protected. Now that the cost of the 'protect the hubs' strategy has been estimated, a comparison between cost and benefits can be made. First, a comparison between the 'protect the hubs' strategy and the random strategy is undertaken. The simulation first protects the most-connected node, then the second-most-connected node and so on until the allotted funds ($19,544) have been spent. Next, nodes are randomly selected and protected until the allotted funds have all been spent. Finally the malicious attack simulation is run to see which strategy results in a better return on investment for the allotted funds (Table 7.1). The malicious attack simulation was run 30 times and the worst-case scenario is presented in the table.

Table 7.1   Cost effectiveness analysis of random and hub protection strategies

	Strategy: Random	Strategy: Protect the Hubs
Protected Nodes	4637	276
Non-Infected Nodes	7220	11186
CE Ratio	$2.71	$1.75
% Infected	40%	7%
Protected Paths	18790	41274
Path Multiplier	4.1	149.5
Network Integrity	No	Yes

Adding a cost component to the analysis illustrates that the 'protect the hubs' strategy produces a better return on investment. For the same monetary investment in protection, the 'protect the hubs' strategy resulted in only 7 percent of the network being infected, and for the 276 nodes protected, 41,274 paths to other nodes were de facto protected, a roughly 150× protection multiplier. This compares to the random strategy that allowed 40 percent of the network to be infected and only a 4× protection multiplier. Further, the protection cost per node for the targeted strategy was only $1.77 compared to $2.71 for the random strategy. Also it is important to note that with 40 percent of the network compromised, it becomes disconnected, and large parts of the network cannot communicate with each other; thus the network has lost its integrity. While the 'protect the hubs' strategy does better than a random strategy, are there other strategies that might outperform it? To test the comparative value of the 'protect the hubs' strategy, three other strategies were devised for testing:

- Bottom tier – the least expensive node in the network to protect is chosen, followed by the next least expensive node, and so on until the total funds allotted for protection are consumed.
- Middle tier – the first node not protected by 'protect the hubs' strategy is selected for protection, followed by the next most expensive node to protect, and so on until the total funds allotted for protection are consumed.
- Multi-tier – a node is randomly chosen from the 'protect the hubs' strategy, then another is randomly chosen from the bottom tier, then another chosen randomly from the middle tier, and so on in that order until the total funds allotted for protection are consumed.

The same malicious attack simulation is run with all three new strategies, with 30 runs, selecting the worst-case scenarios for comparison. The simulation runs produced the results presented in Table 7.2.

Table 7.2   Cost effectiveness analysis of competing cybersecurity strategies

Strategy	Protect the Hubs	Bottom Tier	Middle Tier	Multi-Tier
Protected Nodes	276	11028	6861	786
Non-Infected Nodes	11186	11030	8120	10331
CE Ratio	$1.74	$1.77	$2.41	$1.89
% Infected	7%	8%	32%	14%
Protected Paths	41274	7058	9808	37456
Path Multiplier	149.5	0.6	1.4	47.7
Network Integrity	Yes	No	No	Yes

EXPERIMENT 2 RESULTS

The 'protect the hubs' strategy still performs the best of the group, but the bottom tier strategy also produces seemingly good results. This confirms that the 'protect the hubs' strategy is also the most cost effective strategy at a cost of $1.74 per node. The bottom tier strategy results in only 8 percent of the network being infected, just 1 percent higher than the 'protect the hubs' strategy, and a low $1.77 cost per node for protection. This 'protect the small guy' strategy appears to give good results, but a closer inspection illustrates the shortcoming of this strategy. While the bottom tier strategy directly protects a huge number of nodes, 11,028, it leaves the most-connected nodes vulnerable. This is critical because the most-connected nodes are what allow the least-connected nodes to communicate with each other. The least-connected nodes rarely link directly to each other. Thus, with the loss of the top most-connected nodes, the network is balkanized to an incredible degree; this is best seen in a before-and-after visualization of the network in Figure 7.5.

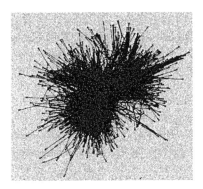
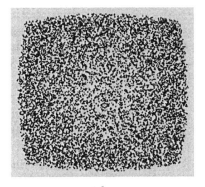

Before   After

Figure 7.5   Before-and-after network visualization of the bottom tier strategy

Perhaps the most interesting result is the relatively good performance of the multi-tier strategy. Utilizing random selection from the other three strategies, the multi-tier approach results in only 14 percent of the network being infected, an almost 50× protection multiplier, a relatively low $1.89 protection cost per node, and results in a network that does not lose its integrity after attack. This is important because the 'protect the hubs' strategy depends on total cooperation of all the top nodes. The difficulty of this requirement is illustrated in the next section.

THE IMPACT OF POLICY ON CYBERSECURITY STRATEGY IMPLEMENTATION

There remains another important facet to this research, an assessment of the impact of policy on the implementation of cybersecurity strategies. How many ASs in the network would fall under US jurisdiction, and would a US policy affecting only US firms be enough to obtain a reasonable level of security? In order to begin examining this issue, the top 350 ASs registered with US addresses were compiled. Next, a protection scenario was run with the most-connected US firm protected, followed by the next most-connected through the top 350 using the strong worm methodology outlined previously. The results of the strong worm algorithm with a US-only protection strategy were then plotted over the same procedure using the top 350 global ASs. The result can be seen in Figure 7.6.

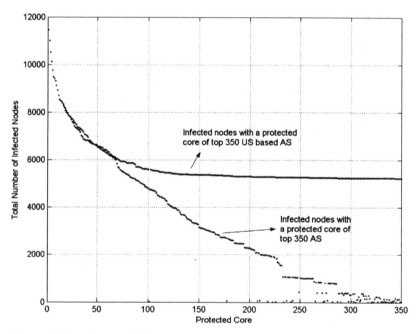

Figure 7.6   US vs. global protection with the strong worm algorithm

EXPERIMENT 3 RESULTS

The results illustrate similar levels of protection with the US-only strategy through the top 75 ASs, then the global AS strategy begins to protect more ASs than the US-only strategy. After the top 100 ASs, the US-only strategy flatlines with over 5,000 ASs still being infected, while the global strategy continues to decrease and largely contains infections around 275 ASs protected. This finding confirms that a lack of international cooperation will result in more infected nodes than a strategy with international cooperation. The importance of international cooperation is emphatically demonstrated in the 5,000 infected nodes seen in the US-only policy. The result makes a preliminary case that a US-only policy strategy could be an inadequate measure. International cooperation or policies that can influence foreign firm security policies appear to be needed. More specific simulations of policy can be attempted using a similar approach.

FINANCIAL SECTOR VERSUS THE FEDERAL SECTOR

The last experiment examined the issue of jurisdiction, but the same approach can be modified to examine the effectiveness of specific policies. To test this assertion two policies are examined: a federal request for proposal (RFP) strategy proposed by Hunker (2002), and a similar policy targeting the financial services community. Hunker's RFP strategy assumes that if the US government has contracts with a significant number of networks, the basic security requirements built into RFPs could cover a large number of firms and also provide an economic incentive for compliance in the form of increased service fees to cover upgrades. In order to test the federal RFP strategy, the AS graph is utilized to locate all federal government networks, then all their nearest neighbors are calculated. The nearest neighbors are all networks that interconnect with federal government networks to provide connectivity services, and would fall under the RFP regulation. Once this core has been identified, the malicious attack scenario can be run and the cost effectiveness of the policy evaluated. In order to provide a comparison a financial sector policy is simulated as well. In this scenario a policy is simulated where the network providers to all US financial institutions have to meet a minimal level of security in order to obtain RFP contracts. The same approach as that used with the federal RFP sector is employed where all US financial institutions in the US are identified along with their nearest neighbors. The financial institutions and their nearest neighbors constitute the protected core, and the malicious attack simulation is run. The results are used to compare the cost effectiveness of the federal RFP policy to the financial institution policy. These results are presented in Table 7.3.

Table 7.3   Cost effectiveness comparison of a federal RFP versus a financial cybersecurity policy

Policy	Fed RFP	US Financial	World Financial
Protected Nodes	390	488	748
Non-Infected Nodes	4,262	5,787	6,849
Cost of Protection	$9,120.00	$7,480.00	$7,966.00
CE Ratio	$2.14	$1.29	$1.16
% Infected	64.5%	51.8%	42.9%
Protected Paths	16,940	22,086	24,308
Path Multiplier	43.44	45.26	32.50
Network Integrity	Yes	Yes	Yes

EXPERIMENT 4 RESULTS

The results of the simulations demonstrate that the financial policy does a better job protecting the network and is more cost effective. The simulation results indicate that the financial policy results in 12.7 percent less of the network being infected in an attack than the federal policy. Further, the financial policy only costs $1.29 per node to implement, while the federal policy costs $2.14 per node to implement. These findings support the premise that a strategy targeting the financial sector results in fewer failed nodes than a strategy targeting the federal government. The likely reason for this is twofold: (1) the financial sector has more connectivity, with 121 connections to other networks versus 79 for the federal sector, and (2) more of those connections are to foreign networks. The federal core connects to 18 (22.8 percent) foreign-based networks, including networks based in Canada, the Netherlands, Japan, Singapore, Korea, China, Taiwan, Jordan and Russia. The financial core, on the other hand, is connected to 36 (30 percent) foreign-based networks, Australia, United Kingdom, the Netherlands, Australia, South Africa, Italy, Switzerland, Greece, Spain, Canada, Korea, Japan, India, Korea, Malaysia, Chile, Slovenia, Bulgaria, Russia, Romania, Philippines, and Panama. Also, the financial network connects to most OECD countries, which the federal network does not. The third scenario in the table further tests the international hypothesis by including foreign financial institutions and their nearest neighbors in the financial network. The inclusion of foreign financial institutions not only decreases the level of infection by 9 percent, it also decreases the per-unit cost of the protection strategy by $1.16. This simulation, in addition to the US versus non-US scenario, makes a strong argument for the value of international cooperation in cybersecurity efforts.

ACQUAINTANCE IMMUNIZATION STRATEGIES

Recently there has been new theoretical support for why the federal and financial strategies could work well as cybersecurity policies. Cohen et al. (2003) found that an acquaintance immunization strategy was an effective method for protecting computer networks and populations with broad degree distributions. The acquaintance immunizations strategy randomly selects a group of nodes for immunization along with all their nearest neighbors (acquaintances). When the acquaintance strategy was tested, it was found to produce a low immunization threshold for populations with broad degree distributions. A low immunization threshold means that only relatively small numbers of nodes in the network needed to be immunized to prevent the infection from spreading throughout the network. Broad degree distributions characterize a wide variety of real world networks including the Internet, the electric power grid, the World Wide Web, friendship networks, email networks, and air transportation to name a few. The implications of the study are useful for many different applications.

The authors focus specifically on human populations and computer networks, finding the biggest advantage of their strategy resulting from not needing to know global properties of the network. In order to effectively immunize the network, one does not need to know which are the most-connected nodes, or any other aspect of the network's structure, for the strategy to be implemented. This facet has obvious benefits for human populations fighting epidemics like AIDS. It is very difficult to identify which members of the population have the greatest number of sexual partners, for both pragmatic and privacy reasons. In computer networks, the advantage is less obvious, the topology of most computer networks is well known, or can be easily acquired. As this chapter has demonstrated, though, getting all nodes in a global network to cooperate can be very difficult for a variety of economic and political reasons. In any heterogeneous network environment, cooperation of all nodes can be difficult to achieve. The acquaintance strategy offers a method for overcoming such cooperation hurdles, and also explains why the financial and federal strategies in the previous section work far better than random strategies.   The federal and financial strategies are in essence an implementation of the acquaintance strategy. Federal and financial ASs are randomly distributed across the AS graph, but are all likely to connect to hubs for transit across the network. When the federal or financial policy leverages its scope to include their big hubs in a protection strategy, the overall resiliency of the network is dramatically increased.

CONCLUSIONS AND POLICY ANALYSIS

The research supports the effectiveness of the 'protect the hubs' strategy and thus has implications for policy with regard to best approaches to cybersecurity and critical infrastructure protection.   Several studies have pointed out the fragility and vulnerability of the Internet to malicious attack (Albert et al. 2000; Callaway et al. 2000; Cohen et al. 2001).   There has been debate as to the best policy approach to the current security shortcomings of the US's information infrastructure.   It has been offered that there are several options for dealing with the current situation, ranging from regulation, market forces, contract law, standards/best practices, insurance, or government mandated procurement requirements (Hunker 2002).   While a full discussion of all the possible interventions for security goes outside the scope of this chapter, the results can shed some light as to the general directions that might bear the most fruit.

Perhaps the most persuasive argument from the results is that universal regulation is most likely an excessive approach to the problem. At the same time, an uncoordinated approach fostering random protection appears to be largely ineffective.   In the case of telecommunications, industry-wide regulation has been most often justified in the quest to provide universal service for a population (Dinc et al. 1998; Tarjanne 1999). The results of this analysis illustrate that the universal protection theoretically offered by regulation of the Internet produces minimal returns in relation to the effort to protect all the networks connected to the Internet.   In fact, returns diminish significantly after the protection of the top 20 nodes in the network with a weak worm and the top 275 nodes with a strong worm, which constitute only 0.17 percent and 2.3 percent respectively of total nodes in the network.

Further questions still remain: how many firms control the top ASs? The top 20 network providers control over 70 ASs, so it is likely that there are not 275 separate firms to deal with. It was not possible to perform this analysis for this research, but it is an important extension of this research that is under investigation.

The results presented in these simulations, in terms of percentages, can be deceiving; while it only requires protection of 2.3 percent of total nodes to obtain a high level of security, the cost of protecting nodes is not equal. The most-connected nodes in the network are large global networks like MCI, Sprint and AT&T. The costs of securing global networks of this size are significant and dwarf the cost of securing smaller campus networks, for example. Needless to say, protection of 2.3 percent of nodes would not equal 2.3 percent of costs.

Even so, the second experiment illustrated that a 'defend the hubs' strategy is also the most cost effective. While the top tier of connected networks is far more expensive to protect than lower connected networks, they are still a more cost effective investment of scarce resources. This indicates that the small number of firms represented by the top 20 or top 275 ASs would seem to point towards public-private partnerships or selective regulation as appropriate means to address the problem. The difficult task is ensuring that as many of the top ASs are protected as possible, as was illustrated when hypothesis 3 was supported through simulation testing. Even with just the non-US networks removed, the level of protection is significantly reduced. Also it remains to be seen if market forces or even public-private partnerships can provide adequate coverage of the top ASs. Selective regulation of the top ASs could ensure coverage, but questions of equity and hampered competition and innovation could arise. Several of the alternative approaches delineated by Hunker (2002) could be answers to the dilemma as tested in hypothesis 4. The testing of the federal RFP approach in this analysis produces a good result, but an even better result is obtained with a similar approach applied to the financial services community. The financial services policy yielded a better result because it involved a more diverse set of international providers than the federal government policy. The result confirms, yet again, the importance of international involvement in a successful cybersecurity policy. The avenue best suited for producing international cooperation remains to be seen, but possibilities include the World Trade Organization, the United Nations, and bilateral discussions and regional economic agencies such as the OECD and ASEAN.

NOTE

1. This project is supported in part by NSF Grant No. ANI-0082287, by ONR Grant No. N000140110617, and by AT&T Research.

8. Diversity as Defense

Chapter 6 made the assumption that a node can always be protected; however, sometimes it is not possible to know how a node will be exploited, thus making it difficult, if not impossible, to protect it. How would one protect nodes in this instance? A review of the literature offers some insights. Recent research, as previously noted, has shown that several critical technological networks are scale-free structures with power law connectivity distributions, such as the Internet at the autonomous system level and the router level (Faloutsos et al. 1999), the World Wide Web (Barabási and Albert 1999; Huberman and Adamic 1999), and physical SDH telecommunications networks (Spencer and Sacks 2003). Studies have examined the vulnerability of scale-free networks, finding that they are resilient to random attacks, but highly susceptible to targeted attacks (Albert et al. 2000). Researchers have also examined the immunization of scale-free networks including the Internet, finding that targeted immunization strategies work well, while random strategies fail to eradicate a virus below an epidemic threshold (Pastor-Satorras and Vespignani 2001, 2002; Dezso and Barabási 2002). These studies have analyzed scale-free networks assuming that all nodes are homogeneously susceptible to attack or infection. Often in real world networks, only subsets of nodes are susceptible to attack or infection in a heterogeneous population of nodes. One example of such a scenario is Internet worms, which are designed to attack/exploit only specific operating systems or platforms. If a node is not running the operating system or platform that the worm is designed to exploit, then it cannot affect it. The same is true for a wide variety of vulnerabilities of platform-specific attacks, including many denial of service attacks. This leaves the problem of determining what level of diversity in node types is needed so that any one malicious attack won't cause a catastrophic failure of the network. It is important to point out that worms and denial of service attacks require two different methodologies to model. First, a methodology appropriate to denial of service attacks will be presented, followed by a methodology appropriate to worm attack. To test this research question, it is useful to give some background on homogeneity, what causes it, and the debate over the threats of monocultures before describing the methodology.

ECONOMIC DRIVERS OF HOMOGENEITY

A single vendor dominates many real world technology systems and networks, and this phenomenon often results in highly homogeneous networks. For example Cisco systems accounts for 85.5 percent of the global router market and Microsoft accounts for 97.34 percent of the global operating system connected to the Internet (Collins 2002; Onestat 2003). In homogeneous technology networks, the vast majority of nodes connected to the network all run on the same platform or are built by the same vendor. Building networks where all nodes are homogeneous introduces several economic efficiencies to the network; technicians only need to be trained on one system, upgrades can be done universally at one time, and systems can be bought in larger bulk, allowing per unit cost savings. To quote Aucsmith (2003) 'Diversity has a cost. Enterprises have standardized on specific computer hardware and software to reduce procurement, operation, and maintenance costs' (p.17).

This explains why it would be economical for one network to be homogeneous, but the Internet connects many networks together. Why then are so many networks homogeneous across the spectrum of the Internet? One explanation is an adaptation of Arthur's (1989) theory of increasing returns. The fundamental premise behind increasing returns is that in a competitive market environment, as technologies are adopted, there is an accumulation of increasing returns as more individuals select one technology over another. In simpler terms, it is the tendency for technologies that are ahead to get further ahead, and technologies that lose advantage, to lose further advantage (Arthur 1996). The process by which a particular technology gets ahead is not always clear:

> the economy, over time, can become locked-in by 'random' historical events to a technological path that is not necessarily efficient, not possible to predict from usual knowledge of supply and demand functions, and not easy to change by standard tax or subsidy policies (Arthur 1989, p.106).

Mathematically, Bianconi and Barabási (2001) describe these winner-take-all networks. They provide a variation of the scale-free model that includes a fitness parameter in addition to the proclivity of new nodes to attach to already highly connected nodes, which results in the power law descriptions described in the introduction. According to Arthur's work, fitness and preferential attachment could result from a wide variety of factors, not just competitiveness of a node. This implies that winner-take-all and scale-free networks might be theoretically efficient, but possibly not operationally optimal, since the technology locked into the network could not be the most competitive possibility. The possibility of this phenomenon could exacerbate the increasing homogeneity of networks, but are homogeneous networks dangerous?

A report delivered to the Computer and Communications Industry Association entitled 'CyberInsecurity – the cost of monopoly' (Geer et al. 2003) makes a case for how Microsoft's market dominance poses a security threat, and in turn has sparked a heated debate on the topic in the media, industry and academia. Specifically, 'The identicality and flaw density in the Microsoft Windows monoculture present clear dangers to national security' (Geer 2003, p.14). Further, Geer delineates that cascading attacks that spread from one user to another across a network by infecting the same computing platform are the greatest risk. Lastly, 'the only answer to the problem is platform diversity' (Geer 2003, p.17). Despite the controversy on the topic there has not been a quantitative analysis of the effects of diversity on resilience to address the monoculture hypothesis. This chapter will examine the overarching question of technology monocultures and specifically address the question of Microsoft.

DENIAL OF SERVICE METHODOLOGY

The methodology of the approach begins with a simulated scale-free router network of 12,000 nodes, in which all nodes are homogeneous. Next, 1 percent of these nodes are randomly changed into a different node type (vendor) and the network is then heterogeneous. At this point a malicious attack will be introduced to the population that only affects the new node type; at this step, that is only 1 percent of the population. After the malicious attack has affected the susceptible population, the number of disconnected nodes and the number of nodes with only one connection is calculated. Next, 2 percent of the nodes are randomly seeded as the new node population and the process is repeated. This process is duplicated at 1 percent intervals until all the nodes in the network consist of the new node type. The results of this procedure are illustrated in Figure 8.1.

EXPERIMENT 1 RESULTS

The number of disconnected nodes in the network increases linearly until 43 percent of nodes are susceptible, at which time there is an almost vertical jump in disconnected nodes. The large jump in disconnected nodes coincides with the crossover with the number of single edge nodes that experience a corresponding steep drop. The combination of steep numerical shift and crossover is indicative of a catastrophic failure in the network. When 43 percent of the population becomes any single one node type, a single malicious attack can cause traumatic damage to the total network. At the 43 percent threshold, there are more disconnected nodes than single edge nodes and large parts of the networks can no longer communicate with each other. The same break point at 43 percent can be observed when the number of disconnected edges is plotted as shown in Figure 8.2, further supporting the rejection of the hypothesis.

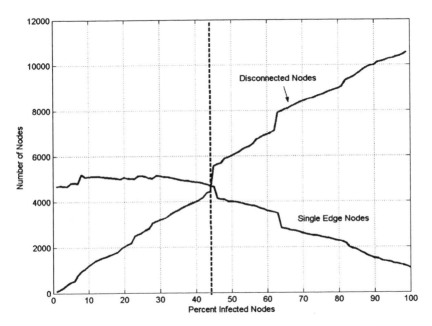

Figure 8.1   Number of disconnected nodes versus size of susceptible population with random seeding

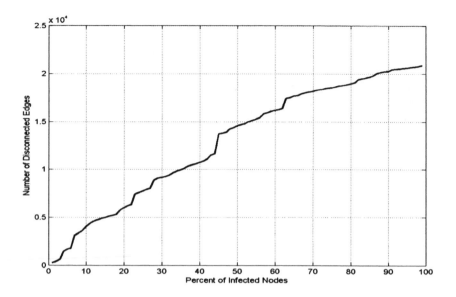

Figure 8.2   Number of disconnected edges versus size of susceptible population for random seeding

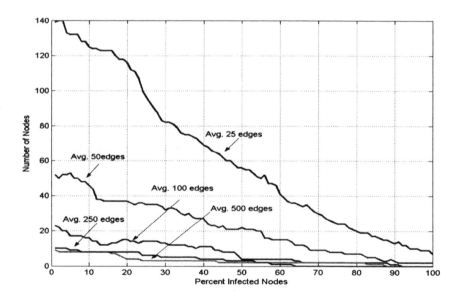

Figure 8.3   Node failures segregated by number of edges for random seeding

Another way to view the degradation of the network is examine the data by segregating nodes according to their number of edges. This was done by constructing a histogram with midpoints at 25, 50, 100, 250, 500 edges per node. The results of this approach are presented in Figure 8.3.

Thus far, the local properties of the network have been examined by investigating the number of disconnected nodes and edges in the network. As the nodes or edges are removed, the connectivity of the network changes and this is not accounted for in just the number of nodes and edges that are disconnected.

One way to determine the integrity of a network is to measure its diameter; as the nodes or edges are removed, the diameter of a network changes, as was done with relatively small networks in Chapter 6. The task of computing the changing diameter of a network is computationally expensive. This problem is even more acute for sparsely connected networks consisting of a very large number of nodes, such as scale-free networks. Recently researchers have used spectral analysis to study the dynamic behavior of networks (Biggs 1993; Alon 1986). Some researchers (Seary and Richards 1997) have used discrete Laplacian to compute the steepest descent or gradient to measure the global connectivity of networks. When either nodes or edges are disconnected, the graph shows the steepest gradient in the direction where there is maximum number of nodes/edge removals. A global property that will capture this behavior is the eigenvalue of a network. Using an adjacency matrix, one may compute the discrete Laplacian as follows: Let A represent an adjacency matrix of a graph G. Let D represent the diagonal matrix formed from node degree of graph G, i.e. $D = \text{diag}(C)$, where, diag refers to diagonal matrix operation on C, the column matrix of node degree is computed from matrix A. Then the discrete Laplacian L is given by: $L = D - A$. Computing eigenvalues of L and studying changes in the eigenvalues of the discrete Laplacian will indicate the dynamic behavior of network G. For random removal of nodes and/or edges, the changes in eigenvalues may be used as a substitute for diameter of sparse networks with a very large number of nodes. One such attempt is shown in Figure 8.4. Incidentally, the jump in the eigenvalue matches the crossover point at 43 percent, as shown in Figure 8.1. This result indicates that a global failure as well as a local failure occurs when 43 percent of the nodes are susceptible, the final evidence for rejecting the 50 percent hypothesis.

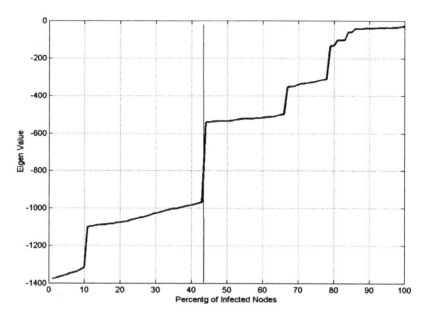

Figure 8.4   Eigenvalues versus size of susceptible population with random seeding

TARGETED SEEDING OF HETEROGENEOUS NETWORKS

Another variation on this procedure is to use a targeted seeding of the population instead of a random seeding. It is important to include this approach since it provides a static comparison to the random approach, which will vary slightly every time it is run. Specifically starting with the most-connected node as the first member of the new species, and the second most-connected, third most-connected, and so on, it proceeds until the least-connected node is turned into the new species. The number of disconnected nodes and the number of single edge nodes is calculated for every 1 percent interval. The results of this targeted approach are shown in Figure 8.5.

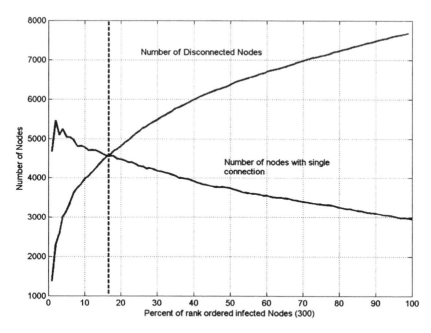

Figure 8.5   Number of disconnected nodes versus size of susceptible population with targeted seeding

The results of the targeted approach illustrate a far more rapid degradation of the network, that is, an exponential increase in the number of the disconnected nodes versus the linear degradation seen in the random seeding. The crossover point with the number of single edge nodes also occurs far earlier, around 17 percent instead of 43 percent, coinciding with the inflection point of the disconnected nodes curve. While the simulation is not realistic it does demonstrate the point that when a node type clusters amongst the more connected nodes in a network it dramatically increases the vulnerability of that network. The corollary to this result would be: the more diversity in the core of the network, the more robust the network. Viewing the node degree histogram plot used with the random seeding approach reinforces this corollary.   The same distribution of average connectivity at 25, 50, 100, 250, 500 midpoints was again used, and is displayed in Figure 8.6.

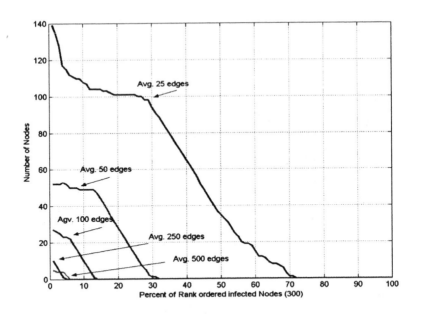

Figure 8.6   Node failures segregated by number of edges for targeted seeding

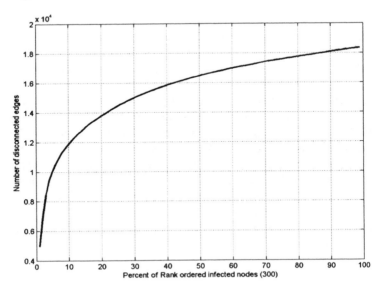

Figure 8.7   Number of disconnected edges versus size of susceptible population for targeted seeding

The shapes of the disconnected node arc for the 25, 50, and 100 edges are all very similar, while the 250 and 500 degrade down to zero almost immediately. The rapid failures of highly connected nodes are directly correlated with the targeted seeding strategy. In the targeted seeding strategy, the most-connected nodes are made susceptible first, so their rapid failure would be expected. The rapid failure of the network in general is linked to the failure of the most-connected nodes first. This is reinforced when the number of disconnected edges is presented, as presented in Figure 8.7.

The targeted seeding results in an exponential loss of edges in the network, as opposed to the linear loss seen in the random scenario. This finding reinforces that the greater the homogeneity in a highly connected core, the more vulnerable a network is. While the router network used for this analysis is simulated, the findings do provide insight into possible vulnerabilities in the current router market. Cisco's market share of 85.5 percent is well above the threshold of 43 percent in a random attack and 17 percent in a targeted attack, and would seem to indicate large security vulnerabilities. The caveat to this is that denial of service attacks on routers do not currently self propagate. Considering that global router maps reach upwards of 200,000 devices it would require coordinated attacks on a very large number of routers in order for a targeted or random attack to be catastrophic. If and when a router self-propagating worm surfaces, this precarious safety balance would be lost, and very significant damage could result. In such a case increased diversity in the router core would be crucial. The greater the diversity of routers in the core, the more possibilities there are for paths around failed routers. Along these lines competition from Juniper and Aveci have increased diversity in the critical core router market, but still only combine to account for 26 percent of the market (Duffy 2003).

WORM ATTACK METHODOLOGY

In the denial of service methodology an attacked node fails and no longer communicates with the network. While this does accurately reflect what happens with a denial of service attack, it does not accurately capture the propagation of a worm. When a worm attacks a system component, it infects it but does not necessarily fail the node. Instead the node stays connected, in turn infecting other vulnerable system components in the network. The computer science literature has examined the propagation of several real world worms and has devised algorithms to simulate their spread (Zou et al. 2002; Ellis 2003; Yang and Yang 2003). Part of the problem with running simulations is finding real world networks with which to test.

To overcome this obstacle, a real world data set is obtained of a zero day worm[1] propagating across a large autonomous system with 16,000 nodes. The packet analyzer utilized for the analysis identified all packets transmitted between IP addresses that were carrying the worm and tagged them with a unique ID and time stamp of transmittal. The IP address to IP address of the worm propagation is then pulled from larger packet capture and sequenced based on their time stamp. Since the data capture isolated IP addresses that were infected, and in turn the sequence the worm propagated, an algorithm to simulate it is not required. Once the routers in the network are identified, it is possible to analyze just the devices that have Microsoft exploits and discover how changing them to non-Microsoft devices would affect the spread of the worm. Figure 8.8 depicts the topology of the worm's propagation across the network after all susceptible nodes have been infected.

The worm propagation also follows a power law connectivity distribution indicating it has the properties of a scale-free network, as seen in Figure 8.9.

The connectivity distribution is rank ordered by the number of connections per IP address in the worm's propagation path, which closely follows a power law connectivity distribution.

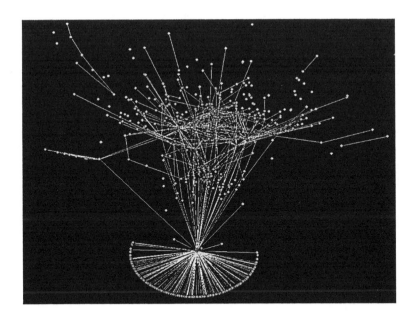

Figure 8.8   Zero day worm propagation visualization

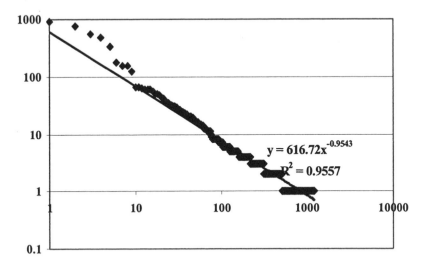

Figure 8.9   Zero day worm connectivity distribution

MICROSOFT DIVERSITY METHODOLOGY

Since the zero day worm only affected Microsoft platforms it is possible to examine the effect that diversifying the infected computing platforms would have on diminishing the damage wreaked by the worm. To do so Microsoft platforms in the worm propagation were identified and 1 percent of them were randomly selected to be changed to a vendor other than Microsoft that would not be infected by the worm and would in turn infect other Microsoft platforms. The worm is then run in time step through the network, and the number of infected machines in recorded. This procedure is run 15 times and the average and greatest number of infections is recorded. Figure 8.10 illustrates the decrease in the number of nodes infected as non-Microsoft platforms are introduced to the network.

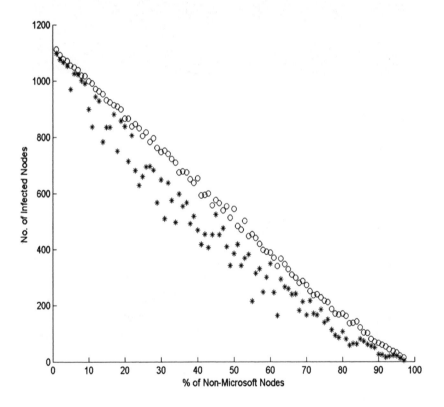

Figure 8.10   The number of infected nodes in relation to the percentage of susceptible machines

The circles are the maximum number of infections over 15 iterations and the stars are the average number of infections. There is no exponential drop in the number of infections as diversity is introduced into the infected network. The decrease is linear; the only protection afforded is from changing the platform - there is no multiplier effect. The worm simply takes another route around the uninfectable machine and still infects the rest of the susceptible network. There is no inflection point where this changes until the entire network is another platform that could in turn be susceptible to its own vulnerabilities. The same trend is seen when the number of infected edges are analyzed.

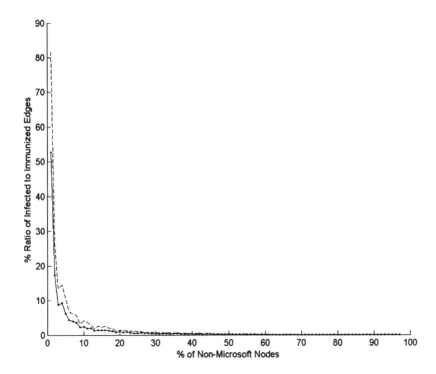

Figure 8.11   The ratio of infected to immune links in relation to the percentage of susceptible machines

A similar linear decrease is seen in Figure 8.12 in the maximum number of infected edges (circles) and the average number of infected edges (stars). Again, there is no multiplier effect seen in the other protection strategies covered in this book. This is further illustrated in Figure 8.11, when the ratio of infected to protected edges is visualized.

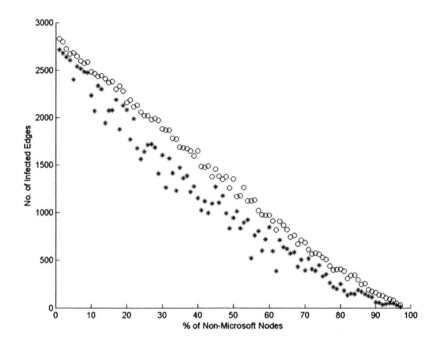

Figure 8.12 The number of infections versus the percentage of non-Microsoft operating systems

The dashed line is the maximum ratio, while the dotted line is the average ratio over the 15 iterations. The graph illustrates the rerouting effect discussed previously. Even though the ratio of infected to protected edges falls very rapidly in a non-linear manner, there is no corresponding drop in the number of nodes infected. The worm still has alternative paths along which to infect the rest of the susceptible population. As seen in the previous simulations, unless the entire highly connected core of the network is protected, then an infection can still propagate throughout the rest of the susceptible network. This is what defeats diversity as a defense strategy against self-propagating malicious attacks. The entire highly connected core needs to be protected, in this case with a vendor other than Microsoft, which would in turn be susceptible to attack, defeating the point of the strategy in the first place.

Ironically, it is this same network property that makes diversity a good strategy when it comes to routers. Since a router fails when it is attacked, it does not stay up and continue to infect other machines. Thus, diversity will make the network more resilient. If there is diversity in the core of a router network, even a relatively small number of routers can keep the network connected and operational. The same property that allows worms to route around non-Microsoft machines and continue to infect the network also allows a router network to stay operational by routing around vulnerable and failed routers. This assertion, though, should be tested in more detail with real world router data sets, but currently goes beyond the scope of this book. In short, the scale-free structure of many data networks has both positive and negative externalities, depending on the nature of an attack.

CONCLUSIONS AND POLICY IMPLICATIONS

The findings of this research illustrate the security issues of reliance on a single network application. In the denial of service methodology, it took only 43 percent of nodes being susceptible to attack for a catastrophic failure to occur. When susceptible nodes were targeted in the highly connected core of the network, the threshold was even lower, at only 17 percent. It is important to note that a simulated router network was utilized for this analysis and a real world network should be used before any definite results are concluded.

The zero worm analysis demonstrated that there was no multiplicative benefit to diversifying operating systems in defending against a real world worm. There was little additional protection afforded by changing operating systems in the worm propagation path; the changed platform was protected but the rest of the vulnerable machines continued to be infected. This was largely the result of the worm's ability to route around non-susceptible machines to infect the vulnerable network. Unless the highly connected core of the network is entirely protected from the worm, it will continue to be vulnerable, as such diversity is by definition an infeasible strategy, since the entire core needs to be homogeneously protected.

In general, the results should not been viewed as hard numbers on which decisions can be based. The approach is useful when questions arise as to whether or not the market share of a particular company in a networked environment is causing possible security vulnerabilities on a macro scale. Results could vary widely by network topology, type of attack, and specific vulnerabilities. The general trend from the results indicates that diversity works well as a defense for non-propagating exploitation of vulnerabilities, but not well for self-propagating attacks of vulnerabilities. In cases where homogeneity does result in vulnerabilities, one must ask 'is antitrust policy an appropriate response?' Antitrust regulation falls under the Sherman Act and specifically, the Supreme Court stated in its Professional Engineers Case, 435 U.S. 679, 695 (1978):

> The Sherman Act reflects a legislative judgment that ultimately competition will produce not only lower prices, but also better goods and services. 'The heart of our national economic policy long has been faith in the value of competition.' Standard Oil Co. v. FTC, 340 U.S. 231, 248. The assumption that competition is the best method of allocating resources in a free market recognizes that all elements of a bargain - quality, service, safety, and durability - and not just the immediate cost, are favorably affected by the free opportunity to select among alternative offers.

In this case, the safety clause would be the part of legislation that specifically applies to network-based applications. When there is a lack of competition and a resulting lack of diversity, this research points to a pronounced negative safety externality. The interdependent and interconnected nature of network-based applications exacerbates the safety issue by affecting constituents who do not use the product or application. In the case of this research, those constituencies are represented by the disconnected nodes and were the non-susceptible nodes in each simulation.

The problem of a growing lack of diversity in networks can be exacerbated by technology lock-in. 'A customer experiences "lock-in" when switching costs exceed the potential incremental value of alternative suppliers' products over its current supplier's product' (Lookabough and Sicker 2003). Lock-in has been a common technology strategy in recent years directed towards growing market share and producing stable revenue growth. When a lock-in strategy aggregates across any one platform, the result can be a non-optimal market creating interdependent security vulnerabilities and negative externalities. Lookabough and Sicker (2003) state that, 'security induced lock-in has resulted in convergence to a stable equilibrium that is not the globally optimal one' and they point towards antitrust policy as one possible policy remedy.

Utilizing national security as a basis to enforce antitrust policy in order to promote competition has historical grounding. During World War II 'national security was a potent weapon in the battle for both public investment and antitrust enforcement' (Hart 1998). Interestingly, US policy to date has gone in the opposite direction with legislative efforts. The Critical Infrastructure Security Act of 2001 (S 1456 IS) states that 'antitrust laws inhibit some companies from partnering with other industry members, including competitors, to develop cooperative infrastructure security strategies.' While closer cooperation among industry actors is vital it is important not to shelve antitrust policy options in the process. This research highlights the benefits of diversity in increasing the robustness of a network and there is a direct link between competition and increased diversity. Antitrust is one policy tool that has been successfully used by the US government to promote national security in the past, but it is questionable if it has relevance to the current security situation.

While antitrust has a precedent for use, it is most likely perceived as an unpopular heavy-handed approach to the problem, as seen in the legislation previously cited. Further, the results of this analysis do not point towards an imminent threat from current technology monocultures. Breaking up the firms that have large monocultures would be unlikely to actually increase security or resiliency. While there is not an imminent threat from monocultures, this picture could rapidly change as attacks become more sophisticated, and increased competition would prove beneficial to both the router and operating system markets. It should also be noted that increased competition in the operating system market could push firms to release software with fewer vulnerabilities for which there is no proper incentive in a monopoly situation, which is the ultimate solution to the problem.

Other more subtle and long-term approaches could be the use of federal procurement policy to encourage or mandate minimal levels of diversity in government networks and computing environments. Spreading this type of initiative to the private sector could include federal research and development funding for firms developing technology to compete with current dominant technologies. Other innovative policy solutions are possible that could increase competition in critical technology areas effectively increasing diversity across the nation's critical information infrastructures. While diversity is an important issue regarding national security, efforts to devise policy and technology to secure network cores and contain self-propagating attacks could prove more fruitful.

NOTE

1. A zero day worm is one that exploits a vulnerability for which there is no patch available to prevent the infection. As a result, there is no preventive action that an end-user can take to avoid being attacked and exploited.

9. Conclusion

The end of the 20th century witnessed a significant change in the nature of economic activity, ushering in a host of euphemisms such as the information age, the digital revolution, the new economy, and the dot com boom. As the economic growth spurred by these dramatic shifts has tapered off, there is a growing realization of the negative externalities from new-found economic efficiencies. Some of the first downsides noted were the increased inequities imposed by the increasing efficiency of the economy, most often encompassed in the digital divide problem (Gorman and McIntee 2003). More recently, a second negative externality has emerged, the creation of public security vulnerabilities. The growing efficiency of the economy came at the expense of growing vulnerabilities to the infrastructures that underpin the economy. These infrastructures have come to be known as critical infrastructures.

THE THREAT TO CRITICAL INFRASTRUCTURE

This book has attempted to perform an objective analysis of issues surrounding the protection of critical infrastructure in the United States. The first question confronted by this work was whether or not there is a threat to critical infrastructure. In recent years many critics have stated that the threat is overblown, especially in areas where loss of life is unlikely, such as cybersecurity. The rationale for this position is that terrorists will focus on attacking targets where loss of life can be maximized. The argument continues that critical infrastructures are built to be resilient, and attacks would not have the high-profile impact desired by terrorist groups. Chapter 3 of this book points to this threat assessment as being naïve; mounting evidence points to terrorist groups, especially Al Qaeda, specifically targeting critical infrastructures, including cyber infrastructures. The skills to exploit critical infrastructures through cyber attacks are being developed by several malicious groups, especially the Russian mafia. Further, there is a high level of vulnerability in these infrastructures even to accidental failures. Lastly, some nation states are increasingly looking to exploit critical infrastructures through information warfare capabilities. The threat is there and by all accounts growing; to disregard the threat because there has yet to be a digital Pearl Harbor is shortsighted at best. A growing and looming threat provides the impetus to examine critical infrastructure in detail to understand how it might best be protected.

THE AGGLOMERATION OF CRITICAL INFRASTRUCTURE

Chapter 4 of this book provided a literature review of material pertinent to understanding critical infrastructure. The general theme of this literature review was laying the groundwork for understanding how private efficiencies can result in public vulnerabilities. Market forces have pushed infrastructures to become increasingly efficient in order to maximize economic return. The result has been agglomeration of infrastructure in large urban areas to maximize economies of scale that create greater efficiency and lower per unit cost of production. This is illustrated analytically by the work of Ciccone and Hall (1996) which examines the correlation of greater density of economic activity with increased efficiency. When these principles are applied to infrastructure networks such as telecommunications, the Internet, and the electric power grid, the result is an agglomeration of connections in urban areas to increase density and efficiency while working in conjunction with the minimization of redundancies to maximize profits and further enhance efficiency. The literature provides evidence of numerous empirical findings supporting such a conclusion ; the agglomeration in urban areas of such critical infrastructures as fiber connectivity, telecommunication switches, collocation facilities, financial services, and information technology firms have all been demonstrated.

Building off the background provided in Chapter 3 and 4, Chapter 5 proposes a set of methodologies for answering sets of interdependent research questions regarding the role of public policy in critical infrastructure protection. Critical infrastructure is a unique problem in that it involves such a wide array of assets and sectors, and as a result no one approach or even discipline is adequate for addressing it. This book has approached the problem as interdisciplinary, and has divided it into a series of interrelated research problems that build upon each other. The first research problem was 'are critical information infrastructure networks vulnerable?' and 'what are the best methods for deciding what the most critical assets in those networks are?' The second was, 'how are critical infrastructure networks structurally different from each other and how are they interdependent?' The third research question asked was, 'if networks are vulnerable, then what are the best methods for allocating scarce resources to protect those networks for increasing return on investment?' Lastly, the question of diversity as defense was addressed. If one does not know what vulnerability an attack will exploit can diversity serve as a viable defense mechanism? Each of these questions has been addressed with different methodologies and data to create three unique but interdependent sets of results and conclusions. The findings from investigating each of the research problems are summarized below.

RESULTS OF TESTING THE VULNERABILITY OF NETWORKS (CHAPTER 5)

The first questions posed by this book were 'are networks vulnerable?' and 'what assets are most critical in those networks?' Chapter 5 of this work dealt with these broad questions by examining approaches for identifying critical nodes and links in a network. Specifically approaches were developed for spatial networks. Since almost the entire critical infrastructure of the nation has a geographic location, these methods are particularly important to develop. The preliminary results demonstrated that incorporating spatial and distance variables improves the ability of an algorithm to identify the most critical nodes in a network. These results supported that an algorithm based on Euclidean distance would produce the best results of the set of tested algorithms. The experiment also illustrated that increased interconnection of IP backbone networks results in greater network resilience. This result again demonstrates the tension between private efficiency and security; less interconnection is cheaper, but also results in less resiliency.

This section of the book's analysis also pointed to a shortcoming of mathematical approaches for identifying critical assets in infrastructure. Often, infrastructure networks cannot be decomposed into links and nodes amenable to mathematical analysis. To clear this obstacle, a grid-based approach was developed to identify and visualize vulnerable bottlenecks in critical networks. This approach highlighted that areas of vulnerability are found in areas of low population. This finding is of particular importance because it illustrates that networks are vulnerable in places other than hubs, which are primarily located in dense metropolitan areas (Malecki 2002). The protection of these critical links is greatly complicated since they often reside in areas of low or no population over many miles.

EXAMINING INFRASTRUCTURE INTERDEPENDENCIES (CHAPTER 6)

Once vulnerability can be quantified it is important to begin to examine how critical infrastructure networks are structurally different and how they are interdependent. Chapter 6 began to examine the issue with a test case analysis of the difference and interdependencies between information infrastructure and electric power. The structure of the two networks closely matched the findings in the literature; the control area interconnection network had an exponential connectivity and the city-to-city IP network had a power law connectivity distribution. When the resiliency of these networks was tested, the findings diverged significantly from what would be inferred from theory stated in the literature. The city-to-city IP network was more resilient to targeted attack than the control area interconnection network. The city-to-city IP network was more efficient (lower diameter) and had a more skewed connectivity distribution, indicative of a higher level of hubbing. The theories put forth in Chapter 4 illustrated that as a connectivity distribution becomes more skewed, the more efficient it becomes, but with the negative externality of being more vulnerable to targeted attack. The result of the experiments in Chapter 6 illustrated that the trade-off between efficiency and vulnerability is not one-to-one. For any one network connectivity distribution, there is a wide array of possible topologies that are possible, some more resilient than others. While there is a general trade-off between efficiency and vulnerability, there are network topologies that maximize resiliency while maintaining efficiency. Even though the possibility exists, there is little understanding of what mechanisms induce it or how they can be incentivized, and this is an important area of further research.

The second part of Chapter 6 examined how the interdependencies of critical infrastructure networks can be examined. There is a multitude of ways that interdependencies can be delineated, and Chapter 6 focused on spatial interdependencies; the geographic commonalties shared by critical infrastructures. For example when critical fiber optic routes and high voltage transmission lines share the same geographic rights of way, an attack, accident, or disaster would affect both. The approach outlined illustrates a method that allows the identification of specific geographic areas where there is a low level of diversity and a high level of infrastructure density for multiple critical infrastructures. The result is the identification of bottlenecks and vulnerabilities that impact multiple infrastructures and where an attack or failure would cause an amplified impact across multiple sectors. This approach demonstrated the correlation between the large magnitude of the 12 August, 2003 blackout and its origin in an area of high vulnerability. The mapping tools are just a first step, and the chapter closed with proposed approaches that allow the quantification of critical components in physical networks, build failure simulations, and apply these tools to interdependent networks.

RESULTS OF TESTING THE ALLOCATION OF SCARCE RESOURCES FOR NETWORK PROTECTION (CHAPTER 7)

Once the critical assets in infrastructure networks have been identified, an efficient protection strategy needs to be devised. The complex network literature points towards a 'protect the hubs' strategy being best, and this work attempted to extend this approach. The second analytical section of the book, Chapter 7, deals with this by evaluating the cost effectiveness of different protection strategies, applied to the Internet's global autonomous system graph. The first experiment found that a protection strategy which targeted the most-connected nodes in a network did significantly better than a random protection strategy, supporting the first hypothesis of this analysis that predicted that a targeted strategy would work better than a random strategy. The targeted strategy was also the most cost effective strategy tested, supporting the second hypothesis of this analysis, that the targeted strategy would provide the greatest return on investment of the tested strategies. The bottom-up strategy that protected the cheapest nodes first also performed very well, but the result was deceiving. While the bottom-up approach protected many nodes, those nodes were not able to communicate with each other, since the well-connected hubs were left unprotected and failed. A middle tier strategy was also employed, but it did not protect many nodes or the hubs in the network, resulting in the worst performance of any of the strategies. Finally a multi-tier strategy was employed that randomly chose a node from the top tier, middle tier, and bottom tier, which resulted in the best performance outside of the targeted strategy. A large number of nodes were protected and enough hubs were protected to allow communication in the network. This result was encouraging, since protecting all the hubs included in the targeted strategy can prove quite difficult.

This difficulty was highlighted in the case of the global autonomous system graph. A scenario was developed where a US-based policy was implemented to protect networks, but the policy only affected networks under US jurisdiction. The result was that after an initial protection benefit, a wall was hit where there was little return for additional US nodes protected, and over half the network continued to be infected by malicious attacks. This result supported the third hypothesis for Chapter 7, that a lack of global cooperation in a cybersecurity policy would result in a higher level of vulnerability in simulated attacks. The high level of interconnectedness of the global Internet meant that malicious attacks could enter the US through international hubs, compromising the network and making a solely US-based defense of limited use. A second policy simulation looked at the comparative cost effectiveness of a US policy that targeted federal government versus financial institutions. The financial institutions policy performed better, protecting more nodes in the autonomous system graph, supporting the fourth and final hypothesis for this chapter, that a policy targeting the protection of financial institutions provides a better return on investment than a similar policy targeting the protection of the federal government institutions. The better performance is in large part due to financial institutions' greater use of foreign providers than the US government. By bringing more foreign providers into the protection strategy, the overall benefits and cost effectiveness increased. When foreign financial institutions were included in protection, the protection benefit increased even further and the per-unit cost of protection actually decreased. This result would seem to indicate that if there were international cooperation among financial institutions in establishing cybersecurity policies, there would be an increased level of protection for all.

RESULTS OF TESTING DIVERSITY AS A NETWORK DEFENSE STRATEGY (CHAPTER 8)

One of the unrealistic assumptions of the protection strategy evaluation in Chapter 7 was that a network could always be protected ahead of time from attacks. Often, new attacks cannot be protected against, and this causes dilemmas in how best to prepare, if at all, and this scenario was confronted in Chapter 8. One approach to protecting networks against unknown attacks is to increase the diversity of the vulnerable components in a network. Most malicious attacks on a network can only exploit vulnerabilities in one platform. Past research has simulated networks assuming that all nodes are homogeneously susceptible to attack or infection. Often in real world networks, only subsets of nodes are susceptible to attack or infection in a heterogeneous population of nodes. The approach taken in this book towards examining a heterogeneous network susceptible to attack tests the effects of different levels of diversity in the network. If malicious attacks can only exploit the vulnerabilities of one type of node, is there a minimal level of diversity needed to prevent any one malicious attack from causing a catastrophic failure?

Testing diversity as a defense strategy produced two distinctly different sets of results. When router networks were analyzed, diversity did prove to be an effective defense strategy, while operating system networks did not benefit from diversity. The reason for the difference was the nature of vulnerability exploits in the two infrastructures. Router vulnerabilities are exploited by denial of service attacks that do not self-propagate; they simply overwhelm the machine, causing it to shut down. As such, a router cannot pass along an attack, thus having diversified routers allows non-susceptible routers to stay operational and route around failed routers. On the other hand, operating systems are most often compromised by self-propagating attacks such as worms. In this case the device does not fail but becomes infected and in turn infects other machines. The scale-free structure of data networks combined with self-propagation of attacks combine to defeat diversity as an effective defense strategy. The highly connected core of a scale-free network allows a worm to efficiently route through the network to infect all susceptible machines even when there is a high level of diversity. The network characteristic that makes diversity work for router networks makes it fail for operating systems. While these results are not universally applicable, the approach presents a tool that is useful in analyzing the effect of diversity in protecting networks and determining reasonable numbers for real world scenarios. The results also point to interesting policy implications.

Diversity at a micro or firm level is very difficult to induce, since running multiple platforms means increased cost in maintenance, training and updating. It may be possible to induce diversity at the macro level through increased market competition, resulting in more technology vendors with smaller market shares and increased diversity among networks, if not within networks. While diversity does have many positive externalities it does not always result in security benefits for all network devices, as seen in the case of operating systems. This, however, does not mean that increased competition in the operating system market would not push firms to release software with fewer vulnerabilities, which is the ultimate solution to the problem.

If one makes the argument that a lack of diversity across the nation's critical infrastructure results in a national security threat, then there is precedent for antitrust action. Antitrust is most likely a heavy-handed solution and other competition-inducing policies such as federal procurement and research and development funding could be effective. The research conducted only proposes a tool to aid decision makers, but the similarity between the simulated scale-free network and real world worm data and several critical infrastructures indicates that inducing diversity through competition could be an effective method for increasing security at the macro level.

ARE PRIVATE EFFICIENCIES CREATING PUBLIC VULNERABILITIES?

The three sets of research problems for this book were set under the general question of 'are private efficiencies resulting in public vulnerabilities?' While the research problems did not test this question explicitly, it is useful at this point to return to the question in the context of the literature discussed and the book's findings. Researchers have found that a wide variety of critical infrastructures (the Internet, World Wide Web, electric power grid, SDH fiber networks, and all three networks tested in this book) form variants of scale-free networks. Scale-free networks capture the competitive forces that drive networks to form efficient structures through preferential attachment.

Barabási's scale-free theory new nodes that connect to a network are more likely to connect to nodes that already have a large number of connections or are more fit (competitive) than other nodes in the network. In this way, scale-free theory expresses mathematically what is illustrated in the economy empirically in the previous section. Agglomeration of infrastructure and network connections in large urban areas results from preferential attachment. The large urban areas become preferential because of the large number of existing connections and their high level of fitness resulting from their greater economic density and resulting efficiency.

This conjecture bears out empirically since the Internet at the router, autonomous system, and city-to-city backbone level all form scale-free networks. Further, physical telecommunication networks like SDH also form scale-free networks, and the electric power grid, airline network and email networks all form broad scale networks. Market forces and competition have done a superb job in creating efficient networks as witnessed by the number of critical infrastructures forming variants of scale-free networks. This efficiency has come at a price: vulnerability. Scale-free networks have been mathematically shown to be quite robust to random failures but highly susceptible to targeted attacks against the most-connected nodes. The research in Chapter 5 expanded these findings to spatial networks, specifically the city-to-city backbone network for many critical communication services. The agglomeration of the most critical nodes in large urban areas, as seen in the results, makes these vulnerabilities all the more alarming.

Accepting that the nation's critical infrastructures are vulnerable means next taking steps to reduce them. The problem is complicated by the fact that the vast majority of critical infrastructure is held privately (CIPB 2002). This privately held infrastructure is governed by market forces, the same market forces that maximize efficiency and unfortunately create vulnerabilities. In order for the private sector to improve the resiliency of these networks, firms must incur an economic loss. Even after an investment has been made to decrease vulnerability, firms must then operate networks in a non-optimal manner, incurring a sustained economic loss. As such, market forces alone will not create less vulnerable networks because they are not profit maximizing. Even if security grows to become a competitive differentiator, the interdependencies of having to interconnect with other networks that decide not to compete based on security will compromise not only the integrity of the overall network but the willingness to invest in security in the first place. It is a stunning case of prisoner's dilemma. These problems are even further complicated by the findings of Chapter 6. Even if the problems of economic incentive are overcome in the United States, without international cooperation protection will be seriously limited.

The efficiency vulnerability trade-off problem is further compounded by market strategies that have promoted the creation of increasing returns through technology lock-in, first mover advantage, and winner-take-all strategies. Information economy strategies have promoted maximizing market share through locking customers into a technology by making switching cost prohibitively high in order to induce their own increasing returns. By taking the benefit of first mover advantage or random historical accident, firms can enjoy winner-take-all network effects, which produce homogeneous networks. The mathematical structure of these strategies is illustrated by Bianconi and Barabási (2001) with a fitness model demonstrating several market outcomes. The problem with these strategies is that they minimized diversity in networks, increasing their vulnerability to attack. Further, as Arthur (1989) points out, this technological path dependency does not always result in the most competitive firm winning, or even in greater economic efficiency. In such a situation, the end is neither efficiency nor security, in short a worst-case scenario. The possible impacts of these path dependencies were demonstrated in Chapter 7, showing that in simulated scale-free networks having a single vendor with more than 47 percent of the network resulted in catastrophic failures in attack scenarios. When a single vendor has a large market share in the highly connected equipment at the core of the network, catastrophic failures occur even more rapidly.

Arrow's impossibility theorem makes the case that it is not possible to have economic efficiency and equity at the same time. A case can be made that the same applies to security – it is impossible to maximize economic efficiency and have a secure network. Specifically as one looks at the properties that make scale-free networks efficient and vulnerable to targeted attack, they are one and the same. The hubbing effect of preferential attachment allows scale-free networks to be efficient – all nodes are a few hops from any other hub, allowing information to hop quickly to any node on the network. The loss of these hubs, as a result, causes a catastrophic failure of the network. The two attributes, efficiency and vulnerability, are intrinsically linked. In this relationship they are very similar to efficiency and equity. In fact, scale-free networks are characterized by power law connectivity distributions, the exact same distribution for which Pareto distributions were used to characterize wealth inequality (Adamic and Huberman 2002). A power law is in essence inequitable; a small minority of nodes have the vast majority of the connections. This inequality is what makes the network vulnerable; when that small minority of the nodes in the network is attacked it results in catastrophic failure. Just as policy faced the dilemma of how to ensure social welfare for a society while promoting capitalism and economic growth, the nation is now faced with the same dilemma in ensuring national security. National security is no longer simply a matter of armed forces, but also involves protecting the economy and its dependence on critical networks, owned not by the government but by private industry. This is a new area and one that cannot be dealt with by market forces alone, but the question remains as to which policy approach will maximize both security and economic efficiency and growth.

FINAL THOUGHTS

This book has made a couple of new contributions to the relevant literature. Chapter 5 provided an extension of network vulnerability analysis to include geographic aspects. Specifically, spatial variables were included in algorithms that well outperformed current approaches. This section of research also developed a new vulnerability heat-mapping tool, which fills a significant gap in the literature for analyzing the vulnerability of spatial networks that cannot be decomposed into nodes and links.

Chapter 7 examined the problems of allocating scarce resources for the protection of networks. This work built upon the research in the complex network literature, providing a new means to calculate the cost effectiveness of cybersecurity strategies. This approach was then expanded to analyze cybersecurity policy and provide cost effectiveness measures for those policies. The cost effectiveness approach for policy analysis begins to fill the gap in the literature for cost benefit analysis of cybersecurity policy demonstrated by Berkowitz and Hahn (2003). Finally, Chapter 8 examined the effectiveness of diversity as a network defense, and what role technology monopolies/oligopolies and increasing returns play in limiting diversity. This analysis provided an important new extension to previous complex network research by examining what happens when not all nodes in a network are homogeneous or equally susceptible to attack. Building heterogeneity of node types into network vulnerability analysis is an important step in creating more realistic analysis.   The inclusion of heterogeneity in analysis also demonstrated the vital role diversity plays in any cybersecurity policy or strategy.

In summary, economic forces have caused an agglomeration of infrastructure in urban areas, and private efficiencies have resulted in public vulnerabilities. Reducing these vulnerabilities while maintaining economic growth and innovation is a difficult path, and there is no single policy remedy. That said, there is a growing body of literature for understanding the nature of vulnerabilities and how they might be most efficiently protected. This research has proposed a suite of new tools to evaluate the growing threat to the nation's critical information infrastructures and has provided a preliminary interface with policy decision-making.

References

Adamic, L.A. and B.A. Huberman (2002), 'Zipf's law and the Internet', *Glottometrics,* **3**:143-50.

Adams, J. (2001), 'Virtual defense', *Foreign Affairs,* **80**(3): 98-112.

Albert, R. and A. Barabási (2000), 'Topology of evolving networks: Local events and universality', *Physical Review Letters,* **85**: 5234-7.

Albert, R., H. Jeong, and A. Barabási (1999), 'The diameter of the World Wide Web', *Nature,* **401**: 130-31.

Albert, R. and A. Barabási (2002), 'Statistical mechanics of complex networks', *Reviews of Modern Physics,* **74**: 47-97.

Albert, R., H. Jeong and A.L. Barabási (2000), 'Attack and error tolerance in complex networks', *Nature,* **406**: 378-82.

Alderson, D., J. Doyle, R. Govindan and W. Willinger (2003), 'Toward an optimization-driven framework for designing and generating realistic Internet topologies', *ACM SIGCOMM Computer Communication Review,* **33**(1): 41-6.

Al-Hayat, M.S. (2003), 'Al Qaeda claims responsibility for power blackout in U.S.!', Dar Al Hayat August 18, http://english.daralhayat.com/ arab_news/08-2003/Article-20030818-14bdd659-c0a8-01ed-0079- 6e1c903b7552/story.html.

Alon, N. (1986), 'Eigenvalues and Expanders,' *Combinatrica,* **6**(2): 73-88.

Amaral, L., A. Scala, M. Barthelemy and H. Stanley (2000), 'Classes of small-world networks', *Proceedings of the National Academy of Science,* **97**(21): 11149-52.

Amin, M. (2001), 'Toward self-healing energy infrastructure systems', *IEEE Computer Applications in Power,* **14**(1): 20-28.

Arthur, B. (1989), 'Competing technologies, increasing returns and lock-in by historical events', *Economic Journal,* **99**, 106-31.

Arthur, B. (1996), 'Increasing returns and the new world of business', *Harvard Business Review,* **74**(4), 100-109.

Arthur, W.B. (1999), 'Complexity and the economy', *Science,* **284**: 107-9.

Atkinson, R. (1998), 'Technological change and cities', *Cityscape: A Journal of Policy Development and Research,* **3**: 129-71.

Aucsmith, D. (2003), 'Diversity has Costs', *IEEE Security & Policy* **1**(6):15.

Barabási, A. (2001), 'The physics of the Web', *Physics World,* July 2001, http://www.physicsweb.org/article/world/14/7/09.

Barabási, A. (2002), *Linked: The New Science of Networks,* New York: Perseus Publishing.

Barabási A. and A. Albert (1999), 'Emergence of scaling in random networks', *Science,* **286,** October: 509-12.

Barbera, P. and R. Rosso (1989), 'On the fractal dimension of stream networks', *Water Resource Research*, **25**(4): 735-41.

Barthelemy, M. (2003), 'Crossover from scale-free to spatial networks', *Europhysics Letters*, **63**(6): 915-21.

Batty, M. (2001), 'Editorial: Cities as small worlds', *Environment and Planning B: Planning and Design,* **28**: 637-8.

Beaverstock, J.V., R.G. Smith and P.J. Taylor (2000), 'World-city network: a new metageography?', *Annals of the Association of American Geographer,* **90**: 123-34.

Bequai, A. (2002), 'White collar crime: A handmaiden of international tech terrorism', *Computers & Security*, **21**(6): 514-19.

Berinato, S. (2002), 'The truth about cyberterrorism', *CIO Magazine*, 15 March, http://www.cio.com/archive/031502/truth.html.

Berkowitz, B. and R. Hahn (2003), 'Cybersecurity: Who's watching the store?', *Issues in Science and Technology*, Spring, http://www.issues.org /issues/19.3/berkowitz.htm.

Berry, B. and D. Marble (1968), *Spatial Analysis*, Englewood Cliffs, NJ: Prentice Hall.

Bhandari, R. (1999), *Survivable Networks: Algorithms for Diverse Routing*, Boston: Kluwer Academic Press.

Bianconi, G. and A.L. Barabási (2001), 'Bose-Einstein condensation in complex networks', *Physical Review Letters*, **86**(24): 5632-35.

Biggs, N. (1993), *Algebraic Graph Theory*, New York: Cambridge University Press.

Boardwatch (1998), *Boardwatch Magazine's Directory of Internet Service Providers: Guide to Internet Access and the World Wide Web Vol III*, No. 2. Golden, CO: Mecklermedia.

Bollobás, B. (1985), *Random Graphs*, New York: Academic Press.

Branscomb, L. (forthcoming), 'Protecting civil society from terrorism: The search for a sustainable strategy' *Technology in Society*, **26**(2-3): 271-85.

Cairncross, F. (1997), *The Death of Distance*, Boston: Harvard Business School Press.

Callaway, D.S., M.E.J. Newman, S.H. Strogatz and D.J. Watts (2000), 'Network robustness and fragility: percolation on random graphs', *Physical Review Letters*, **85**:25.

Cavanaugh, J. (1998), *Frame Relay Applications: Business and Technology Case Studies*, New York: Morgan Kaufmann.

Chen, L. (2003), 'Computational models for defenses against internet-based attacks', unpublished dissertation, Carnegie Mellon University.

Chen, Q., C. Hyunseok, R. Govindan, J. Sugih, S. Schenker and W. Willinger (2001), 'The origin of power laws in Internet topologies revisited', Proceedings of IEEE Infocom 2002.

Christaller, W. (1933), *Central Places in Southern Germany*, Jena, Germany: Fischer, (English Translation by C.W. Baskin, London: Prentice Hall, 1966).

Ciccone, A. and R.E. Hall (1996), 'Productivity and the density of economic activity', *The American Economic Review*, **86**: 54-70.

CIPB (2002), *The National Strategy to Secure Cyberspace*, Washington, DC: Whitehouse Critical Infrastructure Protection Board, http://www.whitehouse.gov/pcipb/.

Cliff, A., P. Haggett and K. Ord (1979), 'Graph theory and geography', in R. Wilson and L. Beineke (eds), *Applications of Graph Theory*, London: Academic Press.

Coffman, K.G. and A.M. Odlyzko (1998), 'The size and growth rate of the Internet', *First Monday*, **3**(10), http://firstmonday.org/issues/issue3_10/Coffman/index.html.

Cohen, R., K. Erez, D. ben-Avraham and S. Havlin (2001), 'Breakdown of the Internet under intentional attack', *Physical Review Letters*, **86**(16).

Cohen, R., K. Erez, D. ben-Avraham and S. Havlin (2003), 'Efficient immunization strategies for computer networks and populations', *Physical Review Letters*, **91**(24).

Collins, J. (2002), 'Dominant Cisco grows router market share', *Personal Computer World*, http://www.pcw.co.uk/News/1131853.

Dean, J. (2002), 'Report stresses management's role in boosting cybersecurity', http://www.govexec.com/dailyfed/0202/021402j1.htm.

Dezso, Z. and A.L. Barabási (2002), 'Halting viruses in scale-free networks', *Physical Review*, E 65: 055103 (R).

Dinc, M., K.E. Haynes, R.R. Stough and S. Yilmaz (1998), 'Regional universal telecommunication service provisions in the US-Efficiency versus penetration', *Telecommunications Policy*, **22**(6): 541-53.

DOJ (2001), 'Press Release', http://www.usdoj.gov/usao/cac/pr2001/104.html.

Duffy, J. (2003), 'Cisco's loss is Juniper's gain', *Computerworld*, http://www.computerworld.com.au/index.php/id;1779513751;relcomp;1.

Economist, The (2003), 'Fighting the worms of mass destruction', *The Economist*, 26 November, http://www.economist.co.uk/science/displayStory.cfm?story_id=2246018.

Ellis, D. (2003), 'Worm anatomy and model', Proceedings of the 2003 ACM workshop on Rapid Malcode, Washington DC.

Erdos, P. and A. Renyi (1960), 'On the evolution of random graphs', *Publication of the Mathematical Institute of the Hungarian Academy of Science*, **5**: 17-67.

Faloutsos, C., P. Faloutsos and M. Faloutsos (1999), 'On power-law relationships of the Internet Topology', *Computer Communication Review*, **29**: 251-60.

FBI (2001), 'E-commerce vulnerabilities', http://www.fbi.gov/pressrel /pressrel01/nipc030801.htm.

FCC (2001), Network Outage Reports, http://ftp.fcc.gov/oet/outage/.

Fonow, R.C. (2003), 'Beyond the mainland: Chinese telecommunications expansion', *Defense Horizons*, **29**:1-8.

Friedman, J. (1986), 'The world city hypothesis', *Development and Change*, **17**: 69-83.

Furnell, S.M. and M.J. Warren (1999), 'Computer hacking and cyber terrorism: The real threats in the new millennium', *Computers & Security*, **18**(1): 28-34.

GAO (2003), 'Critical infrastructure protection: Efforts of the financial services sector to address cyber threats', Report to the Subcommittee on Domestic Monetary Policy, Technology, and Economic Growth, Committee on Financial Services, House of Representatives Washington, DC: US General Accounting Office, http://www.gao.gov/new.items /d03173.pdf.

Gao, L. (2001), 'On inferring autonomous system relationships in the Internet', *IEEE/ACM Transactions on Networking*, **9**(6): 733.

Garrison, W. (1968), 'Connectivity of the interstate highway system', in B. Berry and D. Marble (eds), *Spatial Analysis*, Englewood Cliffs, NJ: Prentice Hall, pp. 239-49.

Geer, D.E. (2003), 'Monopoly considered harmful', *IEEE Security & Policy* **1**(6): 14-17.

Geer D., R. Bace, P. Gutmann, P. Metzger, C.P. Pfleeger, J.S. Quarterman and B. Schneier (2003), 'Cyberinsecurity: The Cost of Monopoly', http:// www.ccianet.org/papers/cyberinsecurity.pdf.

Gertz, B. (2001), 'Al Qaeda appears to have links with Russian mafia', 27 September, *Washington Times*.

Gorman, S.P. (2002), 'Where are the web factories?: The urban bias of e-business location', Tijdschrift voor Economische en Sociale Geografie, **93**(5): 522-36.

Gorman, S.P. and R. Kulkarni (2004), 'Spatial small worlds: New geographic patterns for an information economy', *Environment and Planning B*, **31**: 273-96.

Gorman, S.P. and E.J. Malecki (2000), 'The networks of the Internet: An analysis of provider networks', *Telecommunications Policy*, **24**: 113-34.

Gorman, S.P. and E.J. Malecki (2002), 'Fixed and fluid: Stability and change in the geography of the Internet', *Telecommunications Policy*, **26**: 389-413.

Gorman, S.P. and A. McIntee (2003), 'Tethered connectivity? The spatial distribution of wireless infrastructure', *Environment and Planning A*, **35**: 1157-71.

Green, J. (2002), 'The myth of cyberterrorism', *The Washington Monthly*, November, http://www.washingtonmonthly.com/features/2001/0211. green.html.

GRID (2003), 'Grid technology used to hijack PCs', http://www.gridtoday. com/03/0721/101704.html.

Grubesic, T.H., M.E. O'Kelly and A.T. Murray (2003), 'A geographic perspective on telecommunication network survivability', *Telematics and Informatics*, **20**(1): 51-69.

Guttman, B. and K. Elburg, (2002), 'Israel: Cyber terrorism', *Computer and Recht International*, **5**: 156-7.

Haggett, P. and R. Chorley (1969), *Network Analysis in Geography*, New York: St. Martin's Press.

Halsne, C. (2003), 'North Sound 911 Service Repeatedly Targeted', KIRO TV, http://www.kirotv.com/news/2601577/detail.html.

Hart, D.M. (1998), *Forged Consensus: Science, Technology, and Economic Policy in the United States, 1921-1953*, Princeton, NJ: Princeton University Press.

Hayes, B. (2000a), 'Graph theory in practice: Part I', *American Scientist*, **88**(01): 9-13.

Hayes, B. (2000b), 'Graph theory in practice: Part II', *American Scientist*, **88**(02): 104-09.

Holme, P., J.B. Kim, C.N. Yoon and S.K. Han (2002), 'Attack vulnerability of complex networks', *Physical Review*, **65**: 056109.

Howland, M. (1993), 'Technological change and the spatial restructuring of data entry and processing services', *Technological Forecasting and Social Change*, **43**: 185-96.

Huberman, B. and L. Adamic (1999), 'Growth dynamics of the World Wide Web', *Nature*, **401**: 131-4.

Huitema, C. (1995), *Routing in the Internet*, Englewood, CA: Prentice Hall.

Hunker, J. (2002), 'Policy challenges in building dependability in global infrastructures', *Computers & Security*, **21**(8): 705-11.

Kane, M. (2002), 'U.S. vulnerable to data sneak attack', CNET, http://news.com.com/2100-1017-949605.html.

Kansky, K. (1963), 'Structure of transportation networks: relationships between network geometry and regional characteristics', University of Chicago, Department of Geography, Research Papers.

Kephart, J.O. and S.R. White (1991), 'Directed-graph epidemiological models of computer viruses', in Proceedings of the 1991 IEEE Computer Society Symposium on Research in Security and Privacy, **2**: 343-59.

Knox, P.L. and P.J. Taylor (1995), *World Cities in a World-System*, New York: Cambridge University Press.

Kostas, T., M. Borella, I. Sidhu, G. Schuster, J. Grabiec and J. Mahelrs (1998), 'Real time voice over packet switched networks', *IEEE Network Magazine of the Global Information Economies*, **12**: 18-27.

Kunreuther, H., G. Heal and P. Orszag (2002), 'Interdependent security: Implications for homeland security policy and other areas', The Brookings Institute Policy Brief No. 108.

Lakhina, A., J.W. Byers, M. Crovella I. Matta (2002), 'On the geographic locations of Internet resources', http://www.cs.bu.edu /techreports/pdf/2002-015-internet-geography.pdf.

Langdale, J.V. (1989), 'The geography of international business telecommunications: The role of leased networks', *Annals of the Association of American Geographers*, **79**(4): 501-22.

Latora, V. and M. Marchiori (2002), 'Is the Boston subway a small-world network?', *Physica A*, **314**: 109-11.

Lawyer, G. (2003), 'The battle of the bug: Government, industry move to protect Internet from cyber attacks, viruses', http://www.xchangemag. com/articles/1B1front4.html.

Lerten, B. (2003), 'Tower saboteur: I was only pointing out flaws', *The Bend Bugle*, 23 November, http://bend.com/news/ar_view^3Far_id^3D 12260.htm.

Leyden, J. (2004), 'Zombie PCs spew out 80% of spam', *The Register,* **6**(4), http://www.theregister.co.uk/2004/06/04/trojan_spam_study/.

Leyshon, A. (1996), 'Financial exclusion and the shifting boundaries of the financial system', *Environment and Planning A*, **28**(7): 1150-56.

Liang, Q. and W. Xiangsui (1999), *Unrestricted Warfare*, Beijing: PLA Literature and Arts Publishing House.

Lindstron, A. (2001), 'Tunnel Vision?', Broadbandweek.com, http://www.broadbandweek.com/news/010806/010806_news_fiber.htm.

Longcore, T. and P. Rees (1996), 'Information technology and downtown restructuring: The case of New York City's financial district', *Urban Geography*, 17: 354-72.

Lookabough, T. and D.C. Sicker (2003), 'Security and Lock-in', Economics and Information Security Workshop, University of Maryland, http://www.cpppe.umd.edu/rhsmith3/papers/Final_session8_lookabaugh. sicker.pdf.

Losch, A. (1954), *The Economics of Location*, New Haven: Yale University Press.

Lowe, J. and S. Moryadas (1975), *The Geography of Movement*, Prospect Heights, IL: Waveland Press.

Lunev, S. (2001), ' "Red Mafia" Operating in the U.S. - Helping Terrorists', http://www.newsmax.com/archives/articles/2001/9/28/90942.shtml.

Magoni, D. and J.J. Pansiot (2001), 'Analysis of the autonomous system network topology', Proceedings of ACM SIGCOMM'01.

Maine PUC (2003), 'Docket Number 2002243', http://www.state.me.us/mpuc/misctranscripts/2002-243%20080503.htm.

Malecki, E.J. (2001), 'Where is the Internet's infrastructure, and why does it matter?', International Regional Science Association Meeting, Charleston, SC - Department of Geography, The Ohio State University, 1036 Derby Hall, 154 North Oval Mall, Columbus, OH 43210-1361, USA.

Malecki, E.J. (2002), 'The economic geography of the Internet's infrastructure', *Economic Geography*, **78**(4): 399-424.

Malecki, E.J. and S.P. Gorman (2001), 'Maybe the death of distance, but not the end of geography: The Internet as a network', in S.D. Brunn and T.R. Leinbach (eds), *The Worlds of Electronic Commerce*, New York: John Wiley, pp. 87-105.

Malecki, E.J.and A. McIntee (forthcoming), 'Making the connections: A new industry emerges to interconnect the networks of the Internet' *Environment and Planning B*.

McDonald, H. (2003), 'Beijing spies a useful friend in Castro', *The Age*, 27 February, http://www.theage.com.au/articles/2003/02/26/10460641 02910.html.

McWilliams, B. (2003), 'Cloaking Device Made for Spammers', http://www.wired.com/news/infostructure/0,1377,60747,00.html.

Messmer, L. (2003), 'Navy Marine Corps Intranet hit by Welchia worm', *Network World Fusion*, 08/19/03, http://www.nwfusion.com/news/20 03/0819navy.html.

Moore, D., C. Shannon, G.M. Voelker and S. Savage (2003), 'Internet quarantine: Requirements for containing self-propagating code', INFOCOM 2003, http://www.caida.org/outreach/papers/2003/quarantine/.

Moss, M. (1998), 'Technologies and cities', *Cityscape: A Journal of Policy Development and Research*, **3**: 107-27.

Moss, M.L. and A. Townsend (2000), 'The Internet backbone and the American metropolis', *The Information Society*, **16**: 35-47.

Neuman, P. (1991), 'NY area fiber-optic telephone cable severed; extensive effects', *The Risk Digest*, **10**: 75, http://catless.ncl.ac.uk/Risks/10.75.html#subj1.

Neuman, P. (2000), 'Week-long outage after cable cut downs 11,000 phone lines', *The Risk Digest*, **20**: 84, http://catless.ncl.ac.uk/Risks/20.84. html#subj6.1.

Newman, M.E.J., S. Forest and J. Balthrop (2002), 'Email networks and the spread of computer viruses', *Physical Review E*, **66**: 035101(R).

Newman, R. (2002), 'Wall Street worries', *U.S. News & World Reports*, 23 September.

NIST (1995), 'The impact of the FCC's open network architecture on NS/NP telecommunications security', Washington DC: National Institute of Standards and Technology, http://csrc.nist.gov/publications/nistpubs/800-11/titleona.html.

NRC (2002a), 'Making the nation safer: the role of science and technology in countering terrorism', Washington DC: The National Academy Press.

NRC (2002b), 'Cybersecurity today and tomorrow: pay now or pay later', Washington, DC: National Academy Press.

NSTAC (2002), 'Network security/vulnerability assessments task force report', Washington DC: The President's National Security Telecommunications Advisory Committee, http://www.ncs.gov/nstac/NSVATF-Report-(FINAL).htm.

Nyusten, J.D. and M.F. Dacey (1968), 'A graph theory interpretation of nodal regions', in B. Berry and D. Marble (eds), *Spatial Analysis*, Englewood Cliffs, NJ: Prentice Hall, pp. 407-18.

Odlyzko, A.M. (2001), 'Comments on the Larry Roberts and Caspian Networks study of Internet traffic growth', *The Cook Report on the Internet*, 12: 12-15.

O'Kelly, M.E. and T.H. Grubesic (2002), 'Backbone topology, access, and the commercial Internet, 1997–2000', *Environment and Planning B*, **29**(4): 533-52.

Onestat.com (2003), http://www.onestat.com/html/aboutus_pressbox24. html.

Pastor-Satorras, R. and A. Vespignani (2001), 'Epidemic dynamics and endemic states in complex networks', *Physical Review E*, **63**: 066117.

Pastor-Satorras, R. and A. Vespignani (2002), 'Immunization of complex networks', *Physical Review E*, **65**: 036104-1.

Philippsohn, S. (2001), 'Trends in cybercrime-An overview of current financial crimes on the Internet', *Computers & Security*, **20**(1): 53-69.

Platts (2004), Platts PowerMap, Boulder CO: McGraw Hill.

Pollard, J. and M. Storper (1996), 'A tale of twelve cities: Metropolitan employment change in dynamic industries in the 1980s', *Economic Geography*, **72**(1): 1-22.

President's Commission on Critical Infrastructure Protection (PCCIP) (1997), Critical Foundations: Protecting America's Infrastructures, http://www.ciao.gov.

PSERC (2003), 'Public Utilities Commission of Ohio, sequence of events on August 14, 2003', http://www.pserc.wisc.edu/Ohio_Only_Sequence _of_Events.pdf.

Radoslavov, P., H. Tangmunarunkit, H. Yu, R. Govindan, S. Schenker and D. Estrin (2000), 'On characterizing network topologies and analyzing their impact on protocol design', Tech Report 00-731, University of Southern California, Dept. of CS.

Renesys (2003), 'Blackout results in widespread network outages', http://www.renesys.com/news/index.html.

Rinaldi, S.M., J.P. Peerenboom and T.K. Kelly (2001), 'Identifying, understanding, and analyzing critical infrastructure interdependencies', *Control Systems Magazine, IEEE*, **21**(6): 11-25.

Rodriguez-Moral, A. (1997), 'LIBRA – an integrated framework for type of services-based adaptive routing in the Internet and intranets', *Bell Labs Technical Journal*, **2**(2) (Spring): 42-67.

Sassen, S. (1994), *Cities in a World Economy*, Thousand Oaks, CA: Pine Forge Press.

Seary, A. and W. Richards (1997), 'The Physics of Networks', INSNA Sunbelt XVII, San Diego, 13-17 February.

Spencer, J. and L. Sacks (2003), 'On Power-Laws in SDH Transport Networks', IEEE ICC 2003, May, Anchorage, Alaska, USA.

Sturgeon, W. (2003), 'Organized crime behind Sobig - virus expert', http://news.zdnet.co.uk/internet/security/0,39020375,39115886,00.htm.

Taaffe, E.J. and H.L. Gauthier (1973), *Geography of Transportation*, Englewood Cliffs, NJ: Prentice Hall.

Tangmunarunkit, H., R. Govindan, S. Jamin, S. Shenker and W. Willinger (2002), 'Network topologies, power laws, and hierarchy', *Computer Communication Review*, **32** (1): 76-86.

Tarjanne, P. (1999), 'Preparing for the next revolution in telecommunic ations: implementing the WTO agreement', *Telecommunications Policy*, **23**(1): 51-63.

Telegeography (2002), 'Packet geography 2002: global internet statistics and comments', Telegeography Inc: 1909 K St., NW Suite 380 Washington, DC 20006 USA.

Townsend, A. (2001), 'Network cities and the global structure of the Internet', *American Behavioral Scientist*, **44** (10): 1697-716.

Vegh, S. (2002), 'Hacktivists or Cyberterrorists? The changing media discourse on hacking', First Monday, **7**(10), http://www.firstmonday .dk/issues/issue7_10/vegh/.

Verton, D. (2003), *Black Ice: The Invisible Threat of Cyber-Terrorism*, New York: McGraw-Hill Osborne Media.

Warf, B. (1995), 'Telecommunications and the changing geographies of knowledge transmission in the late 20th century', *Urban Studies*, **32**(2): 361-78.

Wasserman, S. and K. Faust (1994), *Social Network Analysis: Methods and Applications*, Cambridge: Cambridge University Press.

Watts, D.J. and S.H. Strogatz (1998), 'Collective dynamics of small-world networks', *Nature*, **363**: 202-4.

Wheeler, D.C. and M.E. O'Kelly (1999), 'Network topology and city accessibility of the commercial Internet', *Professional Geographer*, **51**: 327-39.

Willinger, W. (2002), 'Scaling phenomena in the Internet: Critically examining criticality', Proceedings of the National Academy of Sciences, **99**: 2573-80.

Wilson, J. (2003, 'Blackout: The conspiracy theory', *Popular Mechanics*, **180**(11): 29-37.

Wilson, M. (1994), 'Telephone tectonics: communication and the restructuring of global services production', unpublished paper, East Lansing: Michigan State University, as cited in: R. Atkinson (1998), 'Technological change and cities', *Cityscape: A Journal of Policy Development and Research*, 3(3).

Yang, Y. and C. Yang (2003), 'Modeling the effects of timing parameters on virus propagation', Proceedings of the 2003 ACM workshop on Rapid Malcode, Washington DC.

Yook, S.H., H. Jeong and A.L. Barabási (2001), 'Modeling the Internet's Large-Scale Topology', http://www.lanl.gov/abs/cond-mat/0107417.

Yoshihara, T. (2001), 'Chinese information warfare: A phantom menace or emerging threat?', Strategic Studies Institute, http://www.iwar.org.uk /iwar/resources/china/iw/chininfo.pdf.

Zipf, P.K. (1949), *Human Behavior and the Principle of Least Effort*, Cambridge, MA: Addison-Wesley.

Zou, C.C., W. Gong and D. Towsley (2002), 'Code Red worm propagation modeling and analysis', in 9th ACM Conference on Computer and Communication Security, **11**: 121-38.

Appendix: Wired buildings in the San Diego central business district

Building	Year Built	Rentable Square Feet	Service Providers
One America	1991	569,630	Winstar, Level Red
600 West Broadway			
550 Corporate Center	1990	343,115	Intellispace
550 West C Street			
Emerald Plaza	1990	356,901	AT&T, Intellispace, Yipes
404 West Broadway			XO, Cox, Pacific Bell
Columbia Square	1990	135,686	Unavailable
1230 Columbia Street			
Koll Center San Diego	1989	360,808	MFS Worldcom, Eziaz, Cox
501 West Broadway			
Symphony Towers	1989	528, 869	Cox, Pacific Bell, ICG, AT&T
750 'B' Street			MCI Worldcom
610 West Ash	1985	174,153	MFS Worldcom, Cox
Wells Fargo Plaza	1984	465,427	Cox, Pacific Bell
401 'B' Street			AT&T, Yipes
Imperial Bank	1982	540,413	Eureka, Winstar, MCI, Pacific
701 'B' Street			Bell, Teligent, Cox, AT&T, ART
Bank of America	1982	272,570	Pacific Bell, AT&T, Cox
450 'B' Street			
101 West Broadway Street	1982	385,648	MCI, Worldcom, ICG, Pacific Bell

			US West, AT&T, Nextlink, Cox, ART
First National Bank	1982	528,271	AT&T, Nextlink
401 West 'A' Street			Pacific Bell, Cox
NBC Building	1975	330,173	MCI Worldcom, ICG, Pacific
225 Broadway			Bell, US West, AT&T, Nextlink, Cox, ART
Comerica Bank	1974	336,648	AT&T, XO, Intellispace, Yipes
600 'B' Street			Pacific Bell
Civic Center Plaza	1972	266,954	Winstar, Teligent
1200 3rd Avenue			
110 Plaza	1971	320,200	AT&T, Winstar, Teligent
110 West 'A' Street			MCI, Pacific Bell
Golden Eagle Plaza	1969	432,858	AT&T, XO, Intellispace, Yipes
525 'B' Street			Cox, Pacific Bell
Union Bank	1966	237,066	Unavailable
530 'B' Street			
Chamber Building	1963	167,928	Cox, Pacific Bell, AT&T
110 West 'C' Street			
Washington Mutual			Metrocom, Pacific Bell
			Time-Warner

Index

D

E

F

G

H

I

K

M